Creative Grieving

A HIP CHICK'S PATH FROM LOSS TO HOPE

ELIZABETH BERRIEN

Thank you for your support!

Elizabeth Berrien

RIVER GROVE
BOOKS

This book is intended as a reference volume only. It is sold with the understanding that the publisher and author are not engaged in rendering any professional services. The information given here is designed to help you make informed decisions. If you suspect that you have a problem that might require professional treatment or advice, you should seek competent help.

Published by River Grove Books
Austin, TX
www.greenleafbookgroup.com

Distributed by River Grove Books

For ordering information or special discounts for bulk purchases, please contact River Grove Books at PO Box 91869, Austin, TX 78709, 512.891.6100.

Design and composition by Greenleaf Book Group LLC
Cover design by Greenleaf Book Group LLC
Cover image: ©IStockphoto.com/chuwy

Cataloging-in-Publication data
(Prepared by The Donohue Group, Inc.)

Berrien, Elizabeth.
   Creative grieving : a hip chick's path from loss to hope / Elizabeth Berrien. — 1st ed.
      p. : ill. ; cm.
   Issued also as an ebook.
   1. Grief in women. 2. Bereavement—Psychological aspects. 3. Stillbirth—Psychological aspects. 4. Spouses—Death—Psychological aspects. I. Title.

BF575.G7 B47 2013
155.9/37   2013940719

Print ISBN: 978-1-938416-33-0
eBook ISBN: 978-1-938416-34-7

First Edition

For Ella

Contents

Foreword

This is a story of resilience, strength of the human spirit, hope in the face of loss, and the connection, joy, and gifts that can inevitably be found through grief. Grief is universal, but society has yet to develop the tools and awareness to approach grief as a "normal" experience. There are so many concepts and rules that we each have in our minds about how grief should be handled, what feelings are involved, the stages someone should be moving through, and the time frame we are given to grieve a loved one who has died. The grieving journey is not a one-sided, rigid process of pain, longing, hopelessness, and despair. A devastating loss is not only an ending but also a new beginning.

Through Elizabeth's story of unspeakable loss, we are given insight into an authentic journey from tragedy to triumph. The path she follows is not neat and tidy and predictable as she walks into the unknown. It is beautifully messy. It is scary, uncertain, painful, joyful, surprising, and ecstatic. As her story unfolds, we witness the breaking open of the spirit. Through fumbles and falls, baby steps and giant leaps, growth creatively begins to occur. Unexpected pathways open up before her as she walks forward fully awake and aware of her emotions and experience. We see her evolve from the depths of sorrow to the point of standing at the peak of possibility and, eventually, to become a woman reclaiming her wholeness. This wholehearted journey from loss to hope would not have been possible without The Model of Heart-Centered Grief that is later introduced in this book. Through this model, Elizabeth was able to truly mine the gifts of her grief, which brought her from deep sadness into a place of gratitude. From this place of gratitude, she was eventually able to give back to the world through the lessons of her journey.

The beauty of Elizabeth's story and the heart-centered grief model is that it can apply to anyone. We are often unaware of our innate resilience when moving through difficult experiences. Yet Elizabeth reminds the reader that through trial and error, humor, self-expression, connectedness, community, and personal creativity the grieving process is a completely natural human experience. It may be different for each individual, but no one is truly alone in the experience of grief. This message of connection along with The Model of Heart-Centered Grief have formed the basis for her nonprofit, The Respite: A Centre for Grief & Hope, which Elizabeth cofounded with business partners Mandy Eppley and Cindy Ballaro in the effort to provide hope to others coping with loss. As she moved through grief, Elizabeth recognized that it affected not only her soul but also her mind and body. Therefore, grief is recognized in its holistic form. This perspective brings the reader to a variety of creative grieving activities listed at the end of this book, which address the different levels—mind, body, and spirit—of the grief experience.

May this book offer you encouragement and empowerment as you embrace the meaning of your own grief journey. Elizabeth's story represents a path that many grieving women have the choice to make. It is about listening to your heart, loving yourself through the hardship, and reclaiming the strength of your spirit. By moving forward with awareness and an open heart, incredible gifts and blessings are revealed. Through Elizabeth's voice, and the voices of other amazing women in this book, may you fully take in what resonates with you and apply it to your own sacred experience of grief and growth—your own creative path from loss to hope.

ANDREW HARVEY
Author of *The Hope: A Guide to Sacred Activism*
(2011 Nautilus Silver Award Winner in the category
Social Change)
Founding Director of The Institute for Sacred Activism
Internationally renowned mystical scholar, spiritual teacher,
poet, and novelist

Acknowledgments

This book has brought my spirit so much joy. Throughout my writing I have met the most incredible people, witnessed some of the most beautiful stories of grief and hope, and continually been inspired by my family, friends, and coworkers that make up the supportive community in my life. I cannot thank all of you enough for your generous support. I feel so honored to have witnessed many of the stories from the women who contributed their wisdom to this book.

I want to acknowledge Carol Poteat, a wonderful writer and coach, who provided great encouragement and enthusiasm since the inception of this book. Her ongoing coaching and support helped me share my story with an open heart. I also want to thank my editor, Linda O'Doughda, for treating my story surrounding the grief journey with such compassion, respect, and wisdom.

I am so deeply grateful to Andrew Harvey for his contribution to this book. He has greatly championed my work and encouraged me to put my voice out there for all to witness. Thank you as well to Chris Saâde, the cofounder of The Model of Heart-Centered Grief. I feel blessed to have your beautiful contribution and ongoing support for our work at The Respite: A Centre for Grief & Hope. You each continue to give tremendous gifts to the world through your teachings and offer deep guidance and inspiration to those who are suffering. It is such an honor to know you both.

I also want to give a special thank you to my dad, David Russell, for tirelessly listening to all my book ideas, for sharing his knowledge as a writer, and for helping me through this process from start to end. Thank you to my mom, Patti, who is always encouraging and who believes in everything I pursue. And my sisters, Megan and Jennifer, who have stood by me, uplifted me, and helped me find laughter at times when I thought it wasn't possible. I couldn't ask for better sisters. I will always appreciate the many late nights you sat up with me as I struggled through my early grief. You were my rocks!

Thank you to my daughter Ella and my stepchildren Lauren, Nathan, and Lily for bringing so much love and light into my life. To my husband, Tim, for your love, patience, and belief in me since the beginning of this project. I also wish remember my son Tookie who left this life all too soon. You are forever in my heart and mind, and a part of everything I do. And to the late William Brian Woods, Jr. May your memory and spirit be honored through the work that is being carried forward.

I also want to acknowledge my incredible business partners, Mandy Eppley and Cindy Ballaro, for their heart and soul support for this book. Mandy was the first person who said I should "go for it" and who believed that my story was meant to be told. I am so grateful to have found such beautiful, wise, and courageous women to carry forward our dream for The Respite: A Centre for Grief & Hope. You have each inspired me with your gifts of helping others. May we continue to bring hope and joy to people grieving everywhere.

Author's Note

This book was written with a female audience in mind. However, I want to welcome men who might be drawn to use this book as a resource for their own grief journey as well. Grief and loss are universal; therefore, the feelings and experiences expressed throughout my story are relatable to anyone. My hope is that whoever is meant to read this book will find it and that it will offer some light, creativity, and empowerment on their path from loss to hope.

My Dream Life

Life was pretty simple and predictable for me up until I was twenty-six. I had a rather normal childhood living in a small town called Big Rapids, Michigan, in a home with two parents; two sisters, Jennifer (eleven years older) and Megan (eight years older); dogs (Taffy, Lucy, and Lilly); parakeets (Sunny and Peppy); and a hermit crab (Iggy). I lived in the same house from birth until I was eighteen. I never experienced any major life transitions until I left home to attend the University of North Carolina at Asheville, pursuing an interdisciplinary humanities degree in anthropology, dance, and music.

I really enjoyed my early twenties. I traveled a lot, made lasting friendships, fell in love, fell out of love, lived in the mountains, worked at an independent bookstore, taught at a Montessori school, moved into my first house, and went dancing every chance I got. I had a lot of joy, and my whole life was ahead of me. When I was twenty-four, I met the man who would one day change the course (and purpose) of my life forever.

I married Brian on January 26, 2007, and knew that I wanted to start a family early. In May, I discovered I was pregnant! I was overjoyed. I was so happy that I began to giggle uncontrollably. I vividly remember going to Lowe's right after I found out. I walked into the store feeling elated and thinking, "I'm pregnant and nobody knows yet but me!" Brian and my family and friends were all so excited when they found out.

I ate very healthy foods—mostly organic—throughout my whole pregnancy. I took lots of walks, did prenatal yoga classes and videos, and slept as much as I needed to. I even took a special class called Dancing for Birth® and became a certified instructor since I loved the dance aspect so much. I was in complete pregnancy bliss. I loved shopping at Motherhood Maternity and picking out new pants and shirts as my belly grew bigger. I took pictures every month to show my belly from the side. I woke up happy every day, eagerly awaiting this amazing gift who was going to be revealed to me after nine months.

We decided to find out the baby's sex, and once we learned it was a boy, I decided on the colors green, cream, and brown for his nursery and clothes. Members of both sides of our families threw two wonderful baby showers for us. Before his birth, I had all of his little clothes folded and organized neatly on shelves, his crib put together and made with sheets, toys arranged, and the pack 'n play bassinet filled with diapers and wipes. He was going to be named Tookie after an Australian teammate Brian had worked with during one of his contracting jobs in Iraq. We liked that it was uncommon and fun to say.

I had always liked the idea of doing a natural birth without an epidural. I had friends who had successfully given birth at home in a birthing tub with the assistance of a midwife. I wanted that intimate environment as well. So I found a doctor who had a wonderful reputation based on doing homebirths for nearly thirty years. I also found a great birth doula who helped prepare me for what to expect during labor. I read tons of books on pregnancy and labor, attended birthing classes, and rented a birthing tub as the due date got close. I was prepared!

I had a feeling that my son would arrive right on time, and I was right. I went into labor the day before my due date. I remember excitedly walking through the grocery store after my prenatal exam during which the doctor told me I had dilated a couple of centimeters. The pain of the contractions was gradually starting to get worse, yet I wanted to make my son a birthday cake for his official "birth" day. So Brian and I grabbed some cake mix and a "0" candle to celebrate his arrival. We also grabbed a vegetable plate and power snacks for the doctor, midwife, and doula. I knew it was going to be a long night. I began making the cake while my contractions were still manageable, but by the time the cake was done baking and I was trying to frost it, I began going to my hands and knees during each contraction to handle the pain.

When I felt that the contractions were getting too intense, I called the doula to come over. She brought with her a basket of candles, massage balls, and aromatherapy scents to help calm me. The doctor and midwife arrived soon after.

I ended up laboring for fourteen hours; it was exhausting. As I was about to give birth, the sun was starting to come up. My son's head crowned while I was in the birthing tub. I remember reaching down to feel the softness of the hair on his head. It was an ethereal feeling.

My Nightmares

After Tookie's head came out, he stopped descending. I kept pushing and pushing, but his body was stuck. The doctor quickly noticed that the umbilical cord was stuck around his shoulder—Tookie was very broad-shouldered—which made the descent harder. Once the doctor finally freed the cord from his shoulder, my son fully arrived.

I was so relieved; I didn't realize at first that something was wrong. My first thought was how beautiful he was. I couldn't believe that I had just given birth to someone so perfect. I noticed that he was very quiet but instantly thought, "After a few rubs, he'll be okay." But when the doctor started administering CPR, I realized things were not okay. I went into shock. I remember thinking, "It isn't supposed to happen this way. This is supposed to be the joyful part." I just stared and stared at him as the doctor worked on Tookie for thirty minutes. Eventually Brian said, "Just tell us." The doctor said our son wasn't going to make it, and I immediately burst into tears. My beautiful baby boy, Tookie, was not going to wake up. I took him in my arms and held him as his little body turned cold and blue. My entire world had suddenly turned upside down. My days of a relatively "easy" life were over. I had been inducted into the world of loss. My hopes, dreams, and future crumbled before my eyes.

The months following my son's death were very dark, and not just in the emotional sense. It was the Midwest in the middle of winter, so the days matched my mood perfectly. I slept for several days after his birth. The doctor had left behind a variety of pain pills, sleeping pills, and antidepressants that my husband gave to me daily. My body was sore and it hurt for me to even walk during that first week. I felt I had no reason to wake up in the mornings. After all I had done to prepare for my child, I couldn't even hold him. My arms ached with a longing I can't describe. I remember thinking, "So this is what hell feels like." I questioned the doctor, Brian, the midwife, and the doula a million times about whether anything could have been done. They assured me that everything that could have been done had been done. Tookie had been too far descended for me to have a cesarean when the trouble started. I had to gradually accept that it wasn't anyone's fault even though I wanted someone to blame! I had to go over the story millions of times in my head for the reality to sink in. I fell into a deep depression.

About four months later, I became pregnant! I was happy, of course, but also scared that if something were to go wrong, I wouldn't be able to handle it. In spite of my fears, however, I enjoyed this second pregnancy as much as my first. By the time I was five months along, I felt more confident that things would be okay and enjoyed a baby shower with my sisters and closest girlfriends. When I found out we were going to have a girl, I began dreaming of dressing her up like a little princess and taking her to dance classes. Ella May Sky was born by cesarean on January 10, 2009—six pounds, six ounces and absolutely beautiful.

We soon settled into what finally felt like a "normal" life. But there was one thing looming in front of us—Brian owed the military one last deployment. He had warned me about this when I first met him. As a Special Forces soldier he had done contract work the majority of our time together, so I was used to him being gone for a period of two months, and then coming home for one month. But his final deployment was going to be with the U.S. Army in Afghanistan for about six months. I spent a lot of time trying to mentally prepare for his departure. I knew from the beginning that Brian would be doing a dangerous job. But I naively calmed myself with the thought, "The worst won't happen to me. I'm a good person; I'll somehow be protected from my worst fears." Well, I couldn't have been more wrong!

At one point I remember saying to him, "You can't die because I won't be able to handle it, especially after losing our son." I think he sort of laughed at my impossible demand and said, "Okay, I promise I'll do my best." A belief settled in my mind that because I had already been through the traumatic loss of my son, I couldn't possibly lose my husband too. That would just be insane! So I held strong to that thought as the day came when we had to drive him to the military base in Fayetteville, North Carolina. We tried to keep our good-bye as casual as possible, but as I watched him run to join his team in the airport hangar, I started getting this sick feeling in my stomach.

The last time I saw Brian on screen when we Skyped, he looked entirely different from his normal self. The traumas of war were visible in his face. His hair and beard had grown out, his skin was very sallow, and he could barely keep his eyes open because he hadn't slept in days. He had been up for seventy-two hours helping in the medical clinic where men were coming in with blown-off limbs and eyes hanging out of their sockets. It was surreal to know those things were going on while I was enjoying sunny days hiking in the mountains and walking the streets of Asheville's summer festival. It was a fierce wake-up call to the realities happening in the world.

The last night I spoke with him, my dear friend Michelle came over to visit. She could tell I was stressed, and since she was going to school to become a physical therapist, she offered to give me a massage. So I had a glass of red wine, enjoyed a relaxing back massage, and slept very peacefully that night. Little did I know what I was going to wake up to.

There was something energetically strange to me about the next day. I went to the grocery store to buy more baby food and I remember that a feeling of panic swept over me. Back home, I looked at the clock and it was after one. Brian usually called me around one o'clock every day to check in and tell me he was okay. I knew his unit had left for a three-day mission the day before, so I thought the delay was just because he was busy or still traveling. But as the hands of the clock inched toward four, I began getting increasingly nervous and impatient. The phone finally rang shortly after four. It was a long distance number that I didn't recognize, so I answered it with some confusion. I didn't know the man who was calling. He sounded pleasant at first, and I thought maybe it was someone from the Family Readiness Group calling to check up on my daughter and me. But as he spoke, I could tell he had other news. He very clearly stated that my husband had been seriously injured in a firefight and was being flown to a medical center in Germany. A part of me instantly thought, "Well then, I'll go help him recover and bring him home." But when I asked for the details regarding the wound, the man said, "He was shot in the back of the head."

My knees went weak and my breath got knocked out of me. I fought to keep from falling. He told me I was going to be flown to Germany with one or two of Brian's immediate relatives. I didn't have a current passport, however, so I needed to have a new photo taken and they would issue me a passport once we were all flown to Washington. I remember crying and cursing in anger as I shoved everything for Ella and me frantically into the suitcases. I was screaming, "This can't be happening! I told him not to go over there. I can't believe this. I'm so going to tell him off!"

When Brian's sister Catrina and I finally arrived at the hospital, a group of doctors took us into a private sitting room and explained to us that Brian's head wound was irreversible and that they wouldn't be able to save him. Once again, my world that I had been rebuilding since Tookie's death crashed down around me. I was in disbelief and felt like I was going to be sick. When I finally saw Brian, his body was covered in tubes and lines, and he had two black eyes, a cut lip, and sand all over him from the desert. I lay in a creaky hospital chair next to him and told him I was scared and that I didn't know what to do. I promised him that I would take the best care of our daughter I could.

After an uncomfortable and sleepless night in the hospital, the doctor came in to ask me which of Brian's organs I felt comfortable with him donating. Brian had indicated he wanted to be an organ donor. I had to fight a feeling of panic as I realized time was almost up, and I would have to return home to a different life. I gave them permission to take several of his organs. Simply having to make that decision was unreal and overwhelming. It seemed like I was in an alternate universe as they wheeled him out of the hospital room to the operating room. I felt helpless and removed.

Brian was taken off life support and he died a short time later. I felt completely lost. I knew that somehow I had to be brave. I thought, "How am I going to pick up the pieces on my own? How much more can be expected of me? Haven't I been through enough? What else do I have to prove?"

As I boarded the plane home from Germany, I was terrified of going back to the States. I knew as soon as my feet hit the ground I would have to face the harsh reality and the challenging road of grief that was ahead of me. I knew it was going to be exhausting, tear filled, anxiety provoking, stressful, scary, and life altering. Yet in the midst of all my fears, I kept reminding myself, "But I'm a mom. I have to figure this out. Ella needs me no matter what."

And indeed, as I walked off the plane, I felt like I was on another planet. Every aspect of my life had again changed in an instant. It was just Ella and me now. Even though I knew I had tons of support waiting, I had lost Brian and Tookie, *half of my immediate family*. What now? I would have to begin the true work of my grief journey. I could not sidestep around it or completely avoid it—I had to save my spirit by walking through it.

Nothing in the world could prepare me for the devastation I felt following the double loss of my infant son and husband within an eighteen-month period. I still look back and wonder how I got through it. I felt as if a sword was slicing my heart into little diced pieces after Tookie died. Then I felt like it was being put through a grinder when Brian was brought home in a casket. At both funerals, the only way I could stand without my knees buckling was to have my friends and family physically hold me up. (Why did I choose to wear *heels* to Brian's funeral, anyway? I wouldn't recommend that to anyone.) There were moments when my heart felt so dark that I actually visualized myself jumping into the open grave.

In the ensuing months, the pain changed me physically as well. When I looked into a mirror, there were dark circles perpetually under my eyes, my skin was pale, and my face looked thin. My clothes just hung on me. It was a long time before I even began to recognize myself again. To walk around feeling as though a knife was constantly sticking out of my chest was hard work. All I could think about was how unfair life was to me. Did God hate me? Why me? Did I do something to deserve this? I knew in my heart that I wasn't hated, that I hadn't been a bad person, and that this did happen to other people. In my darkest moments, however, I thought that I alone had been singled out for punishment from a power greater than myself.

I've written this book because I don't want anyone to feel alone on her grief journey. Grief in itself is an isolating experience because no two experiences of loss are alike. Everyone knows what pain feels like, but no one except YOU knows what it's like to lose the unique relationship or special connection that you had with your loved one. Therefore, one thing we can do as social beings is to find others "like us" who have also been deeply wounded by loss. Remember, you are not alone on your journey.

In the beginning of my grief, I would not have survived if it hadn't been for the connection I made with other women in my life who were walking a similar path. The reality that they understood my feelings was enough to get me out of my hole of darkness. I wish for this book to serve as just such a life buoy for you. I wish for it to hold you up in the depths of your despair and to bring you comfort in its honesty, compassion, and wisdom. Whenever your friend, relative, or support person isn't immediately available, please turn to these pages as a source of strength and validity, and to receive creative ideas for your grief process.

In the pages ahead, you will witness my journey in all of its complexity, creativity, and wholeness. Because I have been raw and broken open, I share my thoughts and feelings with rawness and authenticity. I'm grateful that I have walked far enough down my path to share my story, offer compassion, and provide some words of wisdom for you, dear friend. My hope is that my words here will inspire you to keep moving forward, to be gentle with yourself, and to stay strong. As you continue on your healing journey, remember that life always opens a new chapter filled with meaning and hope, especially when you least expect it!

In the Beginning . . . "Get This Elephant Off My Chest!"

I'm either Sleeping Beauty or a walking zombie!

I'm not asleep . . . but that doesn't mean I'm awake.
—AUTHOR UNKNOWN

In the very early days after Tookie's death and again after Brian's, I had a very rough time with sleep. I was afraid that if and when I fell asleep, I would begin to have nightmares in which I was reliving the trauma of my losses. I would often read until my eyes couldn't stay open any longer. Even when I finally did fall asleep, I would wake up about every hour or two.

As you can imagine, I felt very restless much of the time.

I also had a fear of falling asleep alone. After my husband's death, at least one of my sisters would sleep on a couch next to my bed so that if I woke up suddenly I wouldn't panic. This, of course, is not the case for everyone, but I had issues with being alone. I feared that whenever I was by myself, my mind would keep replaying the terrible events. I wanted as many distractions as possible.

When I was staying at my sister Jennifer's house in my early days of grieving, I would keep her and my sister Megan up until 1:00 or 2:00 AM trying to process different thoughts and feelings. I know I wore them out, but it helped me unload a lot of my sadness and anxiety so that my mind could finally shut down. I think a part of me was hoping that my loved ones would come visit me in the middle of the night—although I asked them to please not scare me if they decided to show themselves! But when I was in the depths of my grief, I honestly would have welcomed them as ghosts. One of my young widow friends put it this way: "The most comfort I found was in sleep. I did a lot of sleeping and waiting for my husband to visit me in my dreams."

I was the most tired in the mornings because they usually followed a sleepless night. I would doze off around 4:00 or 5:00 AM and my body would want to stay in bed until noon or later. This made it very difficult to be with my daughter in the mornings. Like a blessing, Jennifer—who is a morning person and works from home—would take the "morning shift" of looking after Ella and eventually bring her to me in bed while I was in the process of slowly waking up. It brought my heart so much joy to cuddle with her and watch her learn new things each day.

It deeply bothered me that I lacked the energy to be fully present with Ella in the mornings. I didn't want to miss anything as her mother, especially since she was all I had. But in that moment, I needed to allow myself rest so that I could spend more quality time with her and truly be present.

I knew that my strength would gradually return; it would just take me a while to get back on my feet. A couple of weeks after moving into my sister's house I decided to hire a nanny because I didn't want to place extra responsibilities on my sister, even though her help was amazing and she enjoyed creating a close bond with Ella, which continues to this day.

Dear Friend,

Grieving is exhausting!! Do not be surprised if you feel the need to constantly sleep. And even when you do sleep, it is often not restful, so you rarely feel truly rejuvenated when you are awake. You feel like a walking zombie. When you open your eyes, the pain of your loss usually feels like a ton of bricks sitting on your chest. You have that, "crap, this is really my reality" moment when you first wake up, reminding you of why you are in bed in the middle of the day or being jolted awake in the middle of the night. Holding the heaviness of the pain in your heart, absorbing the physical shock that your body endures, and having your brain in overdrive from the memory of traumatic events are enough to bring down even the healthiest of us! Give your mind and body a break as they are trying to process what has occurred. Please listen when your body is asking you to rest. Don't fight the natural need to shut your eyes and lie quietly. Sometimes we are afraid to slow down because then the negative thoughts can seep in. But rest is absolutely crucial in helping you acquire the strength to cope with what has happened. This is a time to be gentle with yourself; don't force yourself to the limits. You have been through enough. If you are a parent and have a child or children who need to be tended to, it may help to ask friends and family members if they can babysit so you can sleep in some mornings or lie down in the middle of the day. If you don't get enough rest, the stress will simply end up making you sick.

If you can't shut your mind off to fall asleep, then perhaps try watching some "light" television programs such as one of those wacky reality shows that are always on nowadays. I admit I got hooked on a few of them, and somehow they managed to make me feel better about some aspects of my own life. I could actually sit there and think, "Well, at least *that* hasn't happened to me!" or "Wow, I've handled life's issues way better than that crazy person." Or watch a movie (I preferred comedies) or read a book or magazine to help you focus on something else for a little bit. Just remember: rest, rest, rest.

Love and Light,
Elizabeth B.

HIP CHICK WISDOM

"Don't let someone convince you to hold back your grief. Do what makes you feel best."

—Tiffany K.

Get me off this roller coaster!

> What they never tell you about grief is that missing someone is the simple part.
>
> —GAIL CALDWELL

I COMPARE GRIEF TO riding a loop-filled roller coaster with the highest mountains and longest tunnels you could ever imagine. It's not an easy ride to get through, and at times it makes you feel physically sick. I completely lost my appetite for the first few months after each loss. And I never knew what emotions I was going to wake up with each morning. There was no pattern to my feelings. I was completely unpredictable.

I'd have days when I'd want to lie in bed until three in the afternoon, and then days when I had the energy to get up and get dressed and head out to see some different scenery. I just had to keep reminding myself that I was grieving—I wasn't crazy. These up-and-down emotions were my mind and body's way of trying to process the major events that had upturned my life. I'd have moments when I'd feel almost in complete bliss getting to snuggle with Ella and feeling so grateful for that incredible, pure love between a mother and child. Then there were times when even her happy little face couldn't distract me from the pain in my heart. There was that pervasive feeling that certain links in the chain were missing. This made me grieve for her as well, knowing that she was beginning her own life journey with losses already an integral part of her story.

One of the things that usually set me off was music in the car. I could be having a day where I was seemingly doing all right (meaning my eyes were not puffy and swollen) and then about five minutes down the road on my way to the store, a song would come on the radio that made me break into tears. I'd have to fight to make it the rest of the way to my destination without being blinded by those tears—or crashing into a guardrail! I eventually learned to leave the radio off and just play CDs so I could control the playlist!

I can also remember looking at some photos of me when I'd been pregnant with my son. One second I was smiling at how big my belly had been, and then before a minute was up, I was sobbing uncontrollably. But I didn't criticize myself for seeming out of control. I was allowing the feelings to come and move through me. They weren't killing me, even though they hurt terribly. It was part of what I had to feel in order for the pain to eventually lessen.

I think there were also quite a few instances when I threw my phone across the room. For instance, I remember dealing with a phone company that said I had an outstanding bill from my previous address. I argued with the employee on the other end that there had been a family crisis, and I hadn't even been living there for several months. After going back and forth many times, I finally demanded to speak to a manager. But she would not budge over the money she said I owed for discontinuing service on such short notice, and I finally broke down into tears and tried to explain why I had moved at the last minute. I begged them to work with me. The manager showed no understanding whatsoever and simply said there was nothing that could be done.

I ended up cursing at the lady and yelling at her for having no compassion. She said, "Ma'am, if you don't stop with the language, we're going to have to end this call right now." So I said okay, hung up on her, and threw the phone across the room. I guarantee I am not always that impatient or rude to other people. However, at that point in my grief, I had no filter and very little tolerance for those who were so heartless toward me in my situation.

Throughout my teens and early twenties, I had always been a mediator and a peacemaker. Then, through the course of grieving and dealing with all my raw feelings and impatience with life in general, I became much more outspoken and forward with people. Not that I was mean to anyone, but I made my points clear and spoke with more authority. It was as if I no longer had anything to be afraid of. I had been through the worst. What reason was there to hold back anymore?

Dear Friend,

Whether you end up crying at a cheesy movie one minute or throwing your phone across the room the next, just know that some other grieving woman has probably already done it before. It's easy to feel out of control and as if you don't know how to handle yourself. You may have been a very shy, inward person prior to your loss, and now you have suddenly transformed into a force to be reckoned with. That happened to me in some respects.

There are always going to be moments, whether one year or ten years into your grief, when something will trigger your emotions. It could be a random song that comes on the radio, an emotional movie, a familiar scent, or any other usually sensory experience that triggers a memory of your loss or your loved one. The various emotions you will go through (anger, sadness, anxiety, joy, confusion, peace) will likely be more intense soon after the death of your spouse or child; as time passes, you will become more familiar with them and start to better understand what triggers those feelings.

For instance, a couple of years into my grief, I came across a box of some of my son's things that I had saved from his memorial service. The box included cards, his baby book, hand- and footprints, and a poem. Unexpectedly coming across these items early in my grief would have brought me to my knees. Yet when I viewed the contents of the box those two years later, I was able to sit mindfully with the items and feel sad, but the feeling was not overwhelming. Remember that even after the years start to go by, it's still normal to be caught off guard sometimes and suddenly feel a wave of anger or sadness. This does not make you a crazy person; it makes you someone who is coping with a loss and becoming more familiar with the feelings of sadness that will invariably arise.

Love and Light,
Elizabeth B.

HIP CHICK WISDOM

"From a caregiver's perspective, you can't control the grieving person. What she does isn't always logical, and is often unpredictable. You can give your two cents, but you have to let the person make her own decisions. It's part of the healing process. (Unless she is doing something unsafe, of course!)"

—Jennifer B.

Am I losing my marbles or just in shock?

> When one person is missing, the
> whole world seems empty.
>
> —PAT SCHWEIBERT

IT'S HARD TO DESCRIBE the amount of shock I felt after both my son and my husband died. I literally felt like I was unable to wake from a bad dream. I felt an extreme amount of unease, anxiety, and nausea, along with a variety of other emotions. I believe it was the reaction of my body to the disbelief that was going on in my brain. There were times when the enormity of what had happened overwhelmed me so much that I actually felt numb. I'd start to go through these periods where I felt void of all feeling. I know this is a common effect of grief, but I also struggled with feeling that the numbness was wrong or inappropriate. (Although I admit there were times when I was grateful to feel nothing instead of the tortured ache that normally filled my heart.) One of the few things that brought me out of the numbness was when I spent time with Ella. Yet I still struggled with feeling present all the time.

One of the most surreal moments for me was after I had gone through both losses and I moved in temporarily with my sister. The whirlwind of all that had happened in my life was hard to digest. A part of me could not believe that I was now basically homeless, living in Jennifer's spare bedroom. It was as if the life I had formerly lived was a movie that had been played out.

I remember feeling disengaged when Jennifer was driving me to my first counseling appointment. I literally felt disabled by my grief.

I was terrified to get behind the wheel of a vehicle. I was worried I couldn't remember how to drive properly or be able to focus on where I was going. It also didn't help that I was in a new city. I can remember the rest of the world and cars passing by us as if everything was in slow motion. I couldn't believe that I was in a new place with no home, no real plan, and that there was NO GOING BACK. I could never go back to my life the way it had been before. It was so much to take in that the fear paralyzed me and made me feel sick to my stomach. I remember thinking, "There is no way this can be my life! I'm ready to wake up now!

Despite my inability to fully accept what was happening, I was incredibly grateful (and am to this day) for the help of my family. I know that any of them would have welcomed my daughter and me into their home. Not everyone has a support system like that.

I remember sometimes wondering if I was getting signs or messages from my loved ones who had passed. I'd occasionally hear sounds at night while lying in bed. I remember one time feeling like my ears were ringing as I was trying to fall asleep, and thought I was hearing a variety of voices. I still don't know whether I was dreaming or not. But I think a part of me wanted to connect to the spirit world so badly that maybe I had imagined the familiar voices in my head. I'm not sure what I believe about the afterlife, but I know how much I really wanted to communicate with the other side. Moments such as this did make me feel like I was beginning to lose it. I even used to pinch myself at times to see if I would wake up from the nightmare I felt trapped in.

Dear Friend,

Feeling numb and detached from the world is another normal part of the grief process. It is our body's way of creating a cushion for the traumatic events that we've experienced, which can make you feel like your head is full of cotton. To actually try to wrap your brain around the idea that the person you loved will never be in his or her physical form again is too hard for our human mind to comprehend. It's that ethereal, unreal part of life that we'll never fully understand. Do not feel guilty or worry that something is wrong with you if you let your emotions shut down for a while. However, beware of the thought that because you aren't feeling things intensely you must be "getting over it." We never truly "get over" a loss, but we can move forward and evolve from it. The reality of your loss will impact you differently as time passes, and certain memories that you might have forgotten about may continue to surface over weeks, months, or even years. This is why it is often said that the second year after losing a close loved one (as I've seen with many widows) can be more emotionally challenging than the first year, mainly because the fog that your mind was in throughout the first year starts to lift, and your brain begins to process the loss on a different level.

In my case, the numbness would come and go. Sometimes it fluctuated with the seasons or it depended on what other activities I had going on in my life. Some women stay numb for a long time by throwing themselves into their work or turning to really unhealthy methods of anesthetizing themselves, such as drug or alcohol abuse. In such instances, they never end up fully coping with the loss or traumatic event. Trying to ignore any emotions regarding your loss may result in more pain by creating feelings of isolation. You may feel as if you are constantly trying to hide something. By listening to your feelings, you create more opportunities for connection and personal growth. You can't go around it; you have to go through it. But remember, you don't have to go through it alone!

Love and Light,
Elizabeth B.

HIP CHICK WISDOM

"The grief journey has taught me to be gentle and compassionate with myself and my humanity. Taking time to comfort the scared and exhausted parts of my body and soul has been incredibly important in my recovery. Simple is best for me, and small measures like massage, soaking in Epsom salts baths, and treating myself to soft blankets, robes, and socks have carried me through the toughest times."

—Aimee T.

I don't have to do this alone

> Vulnerability is the birthplace of
> innovation, creativity, and change.
> —BRENE BROWN

AFTER MY SON DIED, I did not consider finding a therapist right away. Instead, I sought help through writing and talking about the experience of my loss with friends and relatives. (Brian was also coping with his own grief, and I knew he didn't feel equipped to handle all of my feelings. He needed support, too, which I wasn't in a place yet to give.) I also had bought a self-help journal that allowed me to think about different questions regarding the aspects of my grief. I spent a lot of evenings sitting at my kitchen table and writing pages and pages of thoughts and feelings in response to the different prompts throughout the journal. Although I did find some relief in this, as I look back on that time, I wish I had turned to a professional counselor right away.

When I first decided to seek professional help, the therapist I consulted was not right for me. She was terse, almost harsh, and her office was very depressing, with its concrete walls, brown carpeting, and a scratchy couch. You would think a therapist would realize the importance of environment! It wasn't a place I felt comfortable in, so after two appointments, I began to look elsewhere.

I became pregnant again before I found the next counselor. That woman was much more inviting and warmer than the first, and I liked her friendly approach. (Plus, the furniture was much more comfortable.) It was only after talking with her that I realized how much I had been holding inside regarding my son's death. Even though I had read several books on the loss of a child and had tried to keep a journal, I couldn't reach the depths of my feelings until I walked into this new counselor's office. I was a little scared of the pain I would feel, but I knew that the pain itself couldn't be worse than the actual experience I had endured.

As I got further into my pregnancy, my counselor always made sure that my feet were up on a footrest, and I felt very nurtured while I was there. I unloaded my anxieties regarding my upcoming delivery and relived the events of my son's death. Despite the tears and anger that came out, I always left feeling lighter than when I had arrived.

My most intense counseling experience happened after Brian's death. I didn't waste any time finding professional support after my return from Germany. Because I was in a new city and felt so unstable when I moved to my sister's, I was fortunate that she took charge of finding a counselor for me. She had heard of this woman by word of mouth and knew that she had a great reputation as a therapist, so she scheduled my first appointment for me.

I remember feeling a sense of relief and comfort that I was going to be seeing this woman. I hoped that I would be able to go there and break down and seek grounded guidance from someone who was already experienced and not afraid of someone else's pain. I had come to realize that my friends and my family could not provide me with this, no matter how much they loved me. Even though they wanted to support me in any way they could, I knew they could not fully go to the depth of the pain with me or have the words that I needed to hear. I had even lost a few friends who could not handle the intensity of what I was experiencing. Some I heard from again much later, and others I did not.

One experience I remember in particular happened only about a week after my husband died. Looking back, I realize now that my friend simply didn't know how to handle a situation involving human loss. But at the time, I was appalled. A day or two before my husband's funeral she sent me an email inviting me to come over to her new boyfriend's apartment complex in the coming weeks to lie out in the sun with her. She thought getting some of the sun's rays might help stimulate some healing and relaxation. My jaw dropped at what I perceived as her insensitivity. I was so infuriated by her message that I wrote her back a long and angry reply describing how I had just recently lost my immediate family and that I couldn't even *believe* she would suggest that lying out by a pool would soothe my sorrows. I knew that I had been harsh in my email response, but I was crushed by how little she understood.

She immediately withdrew from me and did not even show up at my husband's funeral. I have not seen her since. The friends who were strong enough to stand by my side did show up. Some traveled from long distances to hold me up—both emotionally and physically. This was when I discovered who was truly going to stick by me through thick and thin.

I knew it was hard for my friends and family to be able to "go there" to the deep dark places of my grief with me. I felt I would have been putting too much pressure on them to help me heal, or to ask them to go into an uncomfortable zone that they weren't equipped to handle. I knew they would be able to help me when I was needing a good laugh, or wanted to talk about certain memories, but I didn't want to scare them when the floodgates opened or when I felt like kicking and screaming in pain.

When I first walked into my new counselor's office, I was a fragile mess. I hadn't showered in days, and I had on my sweat suit. As I sat in the waiting room, I just stared at the floor; my whole body ached. I was so weak that my counselor had to take my hands and guide me into the room. I had a fleeting sense of hope in my heart when she reached out to me and I saw she had no fear in her eyes. She wore a faint smile, which made me feel welcome. As soon as we sat down, she assured me that with her clients as well as personally she had dealt with all kinds of grief and that she had helped others through the loss of a loved one. This was familiar territory to her and she herself was not immune to suffering.

I knew instantly that I was going to be able to "let go" with this counselor. Her office enveloped me with warmth and comfort. She had beautiful comfy floral furniture, baroque artwork and angels all over the walls, a big soft rug, and lots of windows with natural light pouring in. Most important, I felt safe. I could walk into that room, sink into the big cozy sofa chair, and talk out my sadness and fears for an hour at a time. I always left feeling less weight on my heart and more strength with which to face the world.

Dear Friend,

Each of us has our own unique feelings about seeking support, but I'd have to say from my own experience that seeking personal counseling (as well as finding a support group, which I describe in detail in chapter 2) were the two best decisions I could have made to help myself through the grief process. I know for a fact that I would not be as far along in my healing (and sanity) had I not sought professional mental health resources. I've heard many women say they are skeptical about counseling (or support groups), yet you never know until you try it.

Even if you've tried counseling for other life issues, if you have not sought counseling since the loss of your loved one, it's a great option to consider as you process the ways in which your loss has affected your life and how to go about moving forward. You may not find the one that works for you immediately, but thankfully there are many different therapists with various approaches and personalities.

A few places to begin looking are through Soul Widows (www.SoulWidows.org); The Respite: A Centre for Grief & Hope (www.TheRespite.org); Psychology Today (www.psychologytoday.com); and The Creative Grief Coaching Studio (www.griefcoachingcertification.com).

If there are financial factors involved, ask different therapists you might be interested in meeting with if they have a sliding scale system. Others might be willing to work out a payment plan. Do not let money be the deciding factor in whether or not you choose to get help. By not seeking help, you may spend more money in the long run on less important things! For instance, a woman may say it's too costly to have a therapy session but she spends twice as much on a shopping spree or a salon or spa visit to distract herself from her sadness.

It is important to remember in the depths of your despair that you do not have to hold all your grief by yourself. It is true that your loss is unique to you and that no one will feel it with the same intensity or sense of loss, but the burden of it does not have to be carried without help from others. If you attempt to walk the path without guidance or words of hope along the way, it is easy to become lost and enveloped in your grief to the point where it consumes you.

Counseling can seem frightening to some, especially if you have not tried that route before. Friends and family are wonderful at offering certain types of support, but often they are unable to provide the healing tools or expertise to properly assist you on your journey. Sometimes they can't be there for you because they don't always have the time, even though they wish they did. It is important to consider this as you think of your support system.

It is true that the grief journey can be very lonely, but it is also up to you to decide just how lonely you will make it. It is NOT a sign of weakness to seek the support of others. In fact, it is actually a sign of strength when you admit that the grief is greater than you and that it does not have to be handled all on your own. It may take several counselors before you find one with whom you connect right away. It is something that you will just know. You will feel a connection with that therapist and become comfortable opening up as you build a relationship. The idea of talking to a stranger about your most intimate feelings may feel intimidating to some, but remember that counselors are trained to help people in pain. They actually like to help people in emotional pain! They will not become as engulfed in the pain as some of your family and friends might naturally be drawn to do. Also, a counselor is someone you can yell or scream at without apology or guilt!

A counselor can see the big picture from outside of the pain and offer tools and techniques to properly guide you through the variety of emotions you will move through for a while. Even if you didn't see a counselor in the beginning of your journey, it can still help to see one months or even years down the road. It is never too late to seek support!

Love and Light,
Elizabeth B.

"It's important to feel whatever you are feeling and allow yourself to move through it. But that is the key—to move through and not dwell. It is often difficult to feel grief and not feel some sort of guilt, whether it's 'I should have been there' or 'There should have been something more I could have done.' I believe everything happens when and how it is supposed to and we have to learn to cope with these experiences, no matter how painful. It will be okay eventually, just not in the same way it was before."

—Corri P.

Taking Care of the Whole You (Life Goes On)

You're not puttin' those sweats in the wash are you?

> Nurture is like psychic Wheaties.
>
> —CLARISSA PINKOLA ESTES

f I wasn't living in sweats for weeks at a time, I was wearing a pair of stretch pants with an oversize T-shirt every day after my losses. I literally wanted clothes I could disappear into, that would engulf me in warmth and comfort.

It was particularly challenging after my son died because my body was in its post-pregnancy state, and I had very few pre-pregnancy clothes I could fit into comfortably. It was extremely painful for me to have the extra baby weight and *no baby to show for it*. I had a very hard time honoring the physical changes that I was left with when I did not have a baby to hold and take pride in. Instead, I looked in the mirror and simply felt fat. I thought I had to hide from the world and placed unnecessary shame on myself. I especially felt self-conscious going out in public, so I wore the same couple of pairs of sweatpants and zip-up hoodies for many weeks as I walked and exercised the weight off. It was another thing for me to mourn—the sacrifice my body had made over a nine-month period with no joy at the end as a result.

When my husband died, I remember falling in love with this extra-soft T-shirt my friend Michelle had given me. There was nothing special about the T-shirt: it was light blue and the word "Running" was written on the front in yellow cursive lettering. It was one of those really worn-in shirts that felt so soft I could barely feel it on my skin. I remember telling her how good it felt and she insisted that I keep it. That shirt, along with a pair of yoga pants, became my staple "grieving uniform." A young widow I know told me, "I found comfort in any clothing item that had ever been touched by my husband. His scent brought me comfort (I knew it was only temporary, of course), and I felt close to him again."

Because I was not working and had no place to be, I had the luxury of sleeping in until nearly noon each day and walking around in the same clothes until I lay back down to go to sleep at night. I had Jennifer or the new nanny, Katy, helping with Ella in the mornings, and the rest of the day I played with Ella. I knew none of them cared what I wore each day. It was as if I were an invalid, with visitors coming to call on me in my room now and then. My friends would come in shifts and take turns sleeping on the couch that was positioned next to my bed. It's as if they were taking over for my sisters on couch duty! You would have thought I was dying from some disease and only had a few weeks to live.

About a month or more after I was widowed, my middle sister, Megan, came down from Michigan to visit, and she and Jennifer decided to go out and buy me some new clothes. I had been like a bear in hibernation that had lost tons of weight from not eating. I was sorely in need of some new T-shirts and jeans that would actually fit me. In fact, I was still living out of a suitcase and had a limited selection. So when my sisters came home and surprised me with a bag of goodies from Old Navy, I was thrilled. It was my first venture into wearing "normal" everyday clothes again. It was refreshing and made me feel a little more energized than sitting around in the same thing day after day. Even though I had no special place to go in them, I at least enjoyed wearing my new outfits.

I saw it as a stepping-stone that helped lift me out of my funk a little bit, and it gradually led to my taking care of other aspects of my appearance. I moved on to scheduling a hair appointment shortly thereafter, and I remember feeling rejuvenated after that experience as well. I started to realize how the attention I put into my appearance affected my energy level and my mental attitude.

At some point, I remember hating how pale and sickly I looked since I had hidden indoors for so long, so I decided to visit the tanning bed a few times. (I know it's terrible for you!!) But the warmth and color that it brought back to my appearance helped my mood temporarily, and I was glad to not look like a vampire for a change. I soon switched to a self-tanning lotion because I knew the last thing I needed to add to the tragedies of my life was skin cancer.

It took time for me to care about my appearance again and to develop the energy to even care about what I was wearing. But it had a positive effect on my confidence once I finally took the first step out of those sweatpants.

Dear Friend,

Throughout your time of grieving, you may find that you are drawn to very particular little comforts. If you haven't yet found something tiny that brings you the slightest bit of joy, you most likely will—whether it's a new favorite TV show you become addicted to, an article of clothing you can't take off, a consistent exercise routine, or a daily caffeine or chocolate fix. One of my widow friends shared that she developed an addiction to Starbucks: she had to eat *their oatmeal* nearly every day! It became a routine for her to go there each morning. It gave her a small sense of purpose and added structure to her day after her husband died. Sometimes those little comforts can bring us a new sense of sanity and a little something to look forward to.

You might find comfort in reading an inspirational book each day, or you might develop a routine of journaling each morning or each evening before you go to bed. Maybe you look forward to a warm cup of tea while you sit in your favorite slippers and bathrobe as you read a magazine. Finding small comforts can really bring about a feeling of pleasure, however fleeting it might be. And believe me, a feeling of pleasure or solace can be so hard to find when you are in the depths of your grief. Sometimes it's the little things that help get you through the day. You may think your comforts sound ridiculous to others, but there is nothing ridiculous about finding one little thing to help you feel good in the midst of pain and sorrow!

Love and Light,
Elizabeth B.

"I found comfort in travel, escaping my reality for large chunks of time. I also often say that my dogs saved me. I know I sound like a crazy person, but I had to get up each day, even if it was for just a little while, and care for them. They made me smile, even in the darkest of days."

—Katie E.

What are you eating?! (Are you even eating?)

People think that food cheers you up, that a doughnut cures all ills, but this only works for trivial complaints. When real disaster strikes, food chokes you.

—HELENA DELA

ONE OF THE FIRST things I lost the desire to do after each loss was to eat. I completely lost my appetite for food. Nothing had any flavor. Perhaps my resistance to food stemmed from a personal desire to wither away. I had lost a great deal of my will to live in both circumstances. Eating was just another reminder that I had to keep moving forward—that I was still alive—while my loved ones were dead and would never eat again. However, Ella gave me the motivation to keep going, which trumped any feelings I may have had of giving up. Even at my lowest, she was the one who could get me out of bed. On top of that, my grief kept me so physically drained I was constantly lying in bed and not working up an appetite anyway.

Ironically, after my son's death, the only thing I had any desire at all to eat was sweets. I could have lived on cake or cookies each day. I couldn't have cared less about eating healthy foods or about nourishing my body. I vividly remember the gathering immediately following the memorial service for Tookie. Several different cakes and desserts were served along with the lunch food. The only thing I felt I could stomach was a slice of red velvet cake. Once my dad saw I was interested in that particular type of cake, he saved several more pieces of it for me because at least it meant I would be eating *something*. One of the widows I know told me: "I ate very little right after my husband died, and when I did, I was on what I call the 'white food diet.' Foods that had no color were the only things I could eat. Potatoes, rice, string cheese, and Brie with white wine. This lasted for about three months."

Even getting fluids down was hard, and I became very dehydrated. I didn't start eating well until about six weeks after my son died. My only motivation to begin thinking about a healthy diet again was that I knew I wanted to try for another baby. I started making special "fertility" shakes from an online recipe. Doing so made me feel that I was doing something proactive in trying to move forward with my life. It was a way of giving myself some hope. I also began to notice the added benefits of strength and energy that came with eating vegetables and poultry and fish.

When I was by my husband's hospital bed in Germany, I could no longer breastfeed my daughter because I'd had to leave her behind in the States. I was trying to make do with a breast pump. But my appetite had gone down so much that I knew I was going to be unable to feed her that way once I returned. That was an additional loss I had to endure. The housing unit I was staying in across from the hospital had a fully stocked kitchen, but I couldn't bring myself to eat any of it. I remember the nurses practically forcing me to drink a protein shake as I sat in the tiny white hospital room in a creaky recliner chair. They kept trying to remind me that I needed to keep my strength up in order to travel home and take care of my daughter. They said that Brian would want me to take care of myself and that I needed to remember I had a daughter waiting at home who would need me. I remember thinking as I heard their attempts at encouragement, "Just shut up already. I'm not frickin' hungry!" But I took the can with the straw just to get them to stop hounding me. Those protein shakes tasted like liquid chalk.

In the weeks after my husband's death, I ate little, but I did become entirely hooked on a special espresso drink from Starbucks. I have never been into supporting major food chains and have always tried to buy from local businesses, but from the first day my sister Megan brought me a venti white chocolate mocha, I had found a new love. (She knew coffee had been my favorite addiction since college, and she has a craving for sweet coffee drinks too.) When she introduced me to it, as I was immobilized in bed, lying there with unwashed hair and dried-out skin from so much sobbing. Savoring my first taste of the massive drink, I thought it was one of the most amazing things I had tasted in years.

At that point in my grieving especially, ANY tiny bit of comfort or good feeling was HUGE. I reveled in the coffee's chocolaty goodness as I sipped it intently. How funny that this first coffee after so much sorrow sticks out in my mind as such a strong memory! But that small delight sparked my realization that those little things really were going to gradually pull me back into the land of the living.

It took several months for my appetite to return. I gradually started regaining the pounds I had lost until I was once again at a healthy weight. But it took quite some time before I really began to enjoy food again. Aside from my specialty coffees and occasional chocolate, I pretty much stuck to bread and water. I was like a prisoner in my own self-made cell. By the time Thanksgiving rolled around, however, I began expanding my palette. I do remember eating a pretty good-sized plate on that holiday—just over three months after Brian's death. Once food became more of an enjoyment than a forced necessity, I was able to gain the strength to start doing more walking and exercising again, which also helped my energy level and overall mental state. Regaining my appetite was another sign that I was on the first rung of the ladder in climbing out of the depths of despair.

Dear Friend,

It may take some time for you to regain healthy eating habits after the loss of your loved one. You may be like I was and lose all desire for any type of food, or you might be the opposite and wish to eat everything in sight. Eating food can seem like another chore you have to accomplish as you're trying to make it through each day. As hard as it is to maintain a balanced diet while grieving, being undernourished doesn't help. At least try to make an effort to eat a vegetable, fruit, and source of protein during the day.

Especially drink lots of water! If the waterworks are flowing often, it is very important to stay hydrated. Keep a glass of water within reach at all times. Even if you have a hard time keeping food down, it is essential for you to maintain your fluid intake. Treat yourself as if you have the flu. Your immune system is going to be down early in your grieving, and feeling weak and sick on top of it will only compound the burden of everything else.

It might help to have friends or family bring you soups or smoothies. It might be that you just don't have the energy to cook, but if someone else supplies it for you, you might be more motivated to keep up with your eating habits. One of my friends had several neighbors who brought trays of food to her door on scheduled nights of the week right after the loss of her family member. It helped her to keep up with her food intake since she didn't have to put extra energy into preparing a meal. Even if you don't like the feeling of having others help you, it's worth it for at least a short time! If you don't have people nearby to help with food or getting groceries, then simply heat up dinners or make salads that don't take much time; these are other easy ways to keep energizing foods in your system.

Love and Light,
Elizabeth B.

HIP CHICK WISDOM

"Because grieving is so emotionally and physically draining, it is very important to eat, drink, and take vitamins to nourish your system. Grieving is hard enough without adding physical weakness and exhaustion on top of it!

Start with small portions of food if you need to.
The stronger your body feels, the better you'll
be able to cope with the myriad emotions you
might experience. A healthy immune system will
create greater overall balance."

—Elizabeth B.

Did you really just say that to me?

Ignore those that make you fearful and sad,
that degrade you back towards disease and death.

—RUMI

THERE WERE MANY TIMES, especially in the beginning of my grief, when I turned to someone with a look that said, "What did you just say to me?" I have to say, though, that in comparison to some women I've talked to, the number of ignorant remarks I had to endure was slimmer than what they experienced. Some of the most irritating comments came in the form of, "At least you're still young, so you can have another child" or "You're looking so good today!" Um, excuse me?? I do not need your opinion on my fertility status or the fact that you think I look good at this particular point in time. And I look good for what, by the way? For a grieving woman? For a trip to the grocery store? For a woman who is seething with anger and resentment inside?

It took me a long time to not take comments too personally. I had to develop a thicker skin as time went by or I would've constantly been flying off the handle. I had to say to myself, "These folks are ignorant and don't know any better. If they were standing in my shoes, they would be eating their words right now." I don't think anyone ever spoke to me out of a negative place. They simply wanted to make me feel better yet only succeeded in doing the opposite.

I also had to remember that people can't tell what you've been through simply by looking at you. In general, people often say things they don't mean or that come out the wrong way, so I've learned to ease up on others. I've realized that only I know my true feelings and the depth of what has happened to me. It's not worth my energy to worry about what they do or do not know about my situation. One of my girlfriends who has lost close family and friends put it this way: "When people tell you 'everything will be okay,' and you want to reach out and slap them, let yourself enjoy the thought of doing just that. But realize they are only trying to help."

One of my widow friends came to this conclusion, "Right after my husband passed, I had a dear friend ask when I was going to have children. I will never understand that one! I also had people sending cards saying, 'He is in a better place.' I wanted to scream at them, 'Are you crazy?! He wants to be here with me. He is not in a better place!' It sometimes feels as though people do things to make themselves feel better, not necessarily you."

She also shared, "My mother made a terrible comment one night about dying and being carried out in a body bag. I had gone through an at-home death—the same situation she was joking about. I did not take it well. I typically ignored them or cried when people said inappropriate things. I was so tired of hearing it all. I know they all meant well and truly no one knew what to say to someone in my place. They were doing the best they could."

Dear Friend,

Unfortunately, our society knows so little about how to be with and support a grieving person that it is easy to get hurt when someone's words don't come out properly or the person seems insensitive to your pain. It is one thing if someone is intentionally trying to hurt you, but if you know in that person's heart he or she means well, sometimes it is best to let it go. I have many widow friends who have learned to laugh off people's comments and perceptions. They know that other people can't possibly understand the weight of their words unless they have been in a similar situation.

I think women in general spend too much time worrying about what others think, and grieving can be a time when we feel so vulnerable that any little comment, no matter how harmless, can send us reeling. Sometimes it may be necessary for you to guide those around you as to what is unacceptable to say. Of course, you can't control everyone's remarks, particularly if it's someone you don't really know. But try to consider the intention behind what's being said before taking the comment too personally. After all, no one really knows your reality or your feelings but you. If you find that you're getting caught up in too many negative comments, go connect with your closest support circle, a counselor, or someone else you trust. Such people can help to validate your emotions and give you a safe environment in which to simply be yourself without harsh judgment or insensitivity. This will help your sanity!

Love and Light,
Elizabeth B.

HIP CHICK WISDOM

"Ignoring people's remarks is not always the way to go, but also try not to be too hard on people. They only know what they know."

—Katie E.

HIP CHICK WISDOM

"You'll get a lot of advice from people trying to be 'helpful' after you lose someone close. In my case, my family had opinions on everything: I should be in therapy. I shouldn't be on antidepressants. I should be home with them, not traveling to spend time with friends. On and on and on. But you'll come to realize that the people giving advice haven't been in your shoes, and they don't understand the depth of your pain and how it's manifesting itself. Now is the time to do exactly what you feel is right to get through the day and to eventually heal."

—Faye H.

Reach out to healing experts & hope communities

> We bereaved are not alone. We belong to the
> largest company in all the world—the company
> of those who have known suffering.
>
> —HELEN KELLER

IN ADDITION TO PRIVATE counseling (you'll recall I discussed individual therapy in chapter 1 in the section called "I don't have to do this alone"), I've also found support groups to be healing—just in a different way. My first experience with such a group was after my son died. No one close to me had lost a child before, but through a friend I met a young woman who had also lost a baby. She was so kind as to offer me support through email. I wrote her about my feelings on particularly emotional days, and she was wonderful at validating them. But I knew that I needed more intimate support. I needed to be with other women in a room where all of us could talk about our experiences in a candid manner. I intuitively knew it would make me feel more stable in my feelings and also give me the opportunity to learn about the coping methods other women were using. I felt so isolated and lonely in my little apartment all day. I wasn't working, had moved to a new state after my son died, and had no close friends or sense of community there. I knew if I didn't make some type of connection with others who could understand my pain, I would probably go insane.

I searched online for a child loss support group and soon found one called the "grieving hearts group" near my home. I remember feeling really nervous as I drove to attend the first meeting. My fingers were gripping the steering wheel, and as I walked into the small brick clinical building I felt awkward. I remember coming into a room full of women (and a few men) who were sitting at desks that were arranged in a circle. The people all seemed pretty friendly. Some greeted me with smiles, and others were so sad that I could tell it was hard for them to reach out beyond their pain. I slid into one of the creaky seats and braced myself for what I was about to experience. I instantly started to feel my heart palpitate faster as I took off my coat and set down my purse. I had invited Brian to come with me, but he had told me the last thing he wanted to do was sit among a group of strangers to discuss his feelings. Out of respect for his own healing process, I didn't force him to go. I went for myself.

The woman who led the meeting—I believe she was a nurse practitioner—made it very clear that no one had to feel obligated to share, especially during his or her first time in group, but each person would be expected to start contributing as time went by. I think I was the only newcomer that day, and I remember sitting there with sweaty palms, silent the whole time, feeling more anxiety than I had anticipated. Every time I wanted to add something of my own experience to the conversation, I became tongue-tied. It was almost as if I were back in grade school and had developed a case of stage fright. I was sure that anything I tried to say would come out wrong or sound stupid. I had never been in a situation before where I was about to lay my heart and innermost emotions out on the table for a group of strangers. It was not as easy as I first imagined it would be. I remember thinking, "Why do I feel so self-conscious? I'm twenty-six years old, not twelve!" I realized that I was being hard on myself for not being more articulate but decided that I needed to be more gentle with myself when it came to dealing with my feelings, an idea that was later reinforced by my counselor. It wasn't until my third meeting that I finally mustered the nerve to say something.

I *did* find some encouragement in hearing the other women

describe their angst, pain, anxiety, and fears. I remember distinctly listening to one woman describe the anger she was feeling regarding her post-pregnancy body, and how she felt rushed to get back to her pre-pregnancy shape because she had no baby to show for it. She was having a hard time feeling like herself. I completely understood everything she said and was relieved that I was not the only person who felt that way. I returned to the group several more times before becoming pregnant with my daughter. I know I would have continued to attend additional sessions but for the stipulation that if any of us became pregnant we were asked to find support elsewhere once we started to show because it might evoke great sadness in the other women who were trying to conceive again. I understood this need to "protect" the other women's broken hearts; therefore, for a while I continued solely with individual counseling.

This first support group experience helped prepare me for the widows-widowers group I attended after my husband died. It was still challenging for me to speak in a large group, but I felt so raw in my pain that I didn't care as much about what others thought or whether I sounded like a blubbering idiot! At that point, I felt like my entire body was inside out and that everyone could read my emotions anyway, so why bother to hide any of them? At the beginning of each meeting, the nun who led the nondenominational group would read a meditation and light a candle. It was a sweet ritual that helped me feel grounded in the space. I didn't have the discipline to meditate on my own, so I was grateful to have someone else guide me through it.

The first widows-widowers meeting I attended was only about four weeks after my husband's death. It took me several minutes and many wads of tissue to compose myself so I could finally share my story. I talked about the loss of my son because I felt that it was an extremely important piece that contributed to the amount of pain I was experiencing. I noticed other people around the table sobbing along with me as I spoke. It helped me a great deal to be near other people who "got it." As I continued to attend meetings once a month, I noticed that I was gradually able to connect with the others in the group, no matter what their age or gender. Meetings became another place of safety where I could escape from the "real world" and give full focus to my healing. It felt good knowing that I was taking care of my heart and my sanity.

I became especially close with a woman named Erica. She was my first real girlfriend after I moved to Charlotte, and I can remember the day that she showed up on my sister's doorstep with a chocolate milkshake. I was in my pajamas at the time and was planted in my usual spot—bed. She knew that other than my attending the support group meetings once a week I wasn't feeling up to leaving the sanctuary of my room yet, so she offered to come to me. I can't even describe the comfort that she brought to my heart when she entered my room with that milkshake and a friendly smile on her face. She was about a year into her grief process and was able to just sit and listen to me and offer gentle words of support as I shared my story. I wish for every woman grieving some loss to have another woman's support in that way.

On another visit, she let me ask questions about her own healing process and share my scrapbook album with her. This was the first time I began to truly feel "normal." Here was this other young woman, around my age, who was able to share with me the realities of our altered lives. Thank the powers that be for amazing girlfriends!!

Dear Friend,

If you have never attended a support group before, you may feel very intimidated by the thought of walking into a room of strangers and offering up your personal pain and experience. Support groups are not for everyone, but I think it is important to at least try a group a few times to see what you might be able to get out of it. It may take a few times of attending to feel comfortable in a group, or it might take trying out a few different groups before you find one that feels like "home." Either way, it is always worth a try to see what resources are available in your area and to take advantage of them. It is also another great reason to get out of the house if you are homebound like I was!

Sometimes it takes time to warm up to the group experience. Support groups are created with the idea in mind that all who come are sharing a very personal part of themselves, and therefore respect, openness, and understanding are well established within the group's structure. There is also usually an understanding that not everyone will feel ready to open up during the first visit. This is okay, too, and you should never feel pressured to share if you don't feel ready. If and when you decide to speak, you may experience an amount of relief that you never expected. You may also receive validation from others in the group who are experiencing similar feelings.

As humans, we are social beings. Having a soul connection with others and the ability to share experiences is part of what helps us operate and function at a healthy level. It is also amazing how, in support groups, you lose the feeling of being in a room of strangers very quickly because you are cutting through all the surface details and going straight to the heart of the common issue that's brought you all together.

Support groups are not all doom and gloom either—at least they shouldn't be or they aren't doing their job! Surprisingly, you may find yourself leaving with your stomach and cheeks hurting because you've been able to laugh at something humorous that was said. And that is a good thing. Humor is a great stress release! There will always be plenty of sad tears, of course, but there has to be that element of hope (and balance) or there would be no point in going.

It also never hurts to build a new friendship with a woman who just might show up on your doorstep on one of your most depressed days offering you a chocolate milkshake!

P.S. By the way, unlike private counseling, which usually has a cost attached to it, participation in most support groups is free or by donation. If your budget doesn't allow you to seek a therapist I strongly urge you to find a support group of people in a situation like yours where you can share your story. For support groups, visit www.TheRespite.org, www.SoulWidows.org, or www.SupportWorks.org.

Love and Light,
Elizabeth B.

HIP CHICK WISDOM

"Be open to finding support. Surround yourself with people who let you be 'you,' let you say and do crazy things, and do not judge. Nothing you say is wrong and the right people will know and understand this."

—Katie E.

"Do not hide your grief. It is an honor for those who love you to be there for you."
—Diane S.

Open up to divine inspiration & other spiritual stuff

Spirituality is recognizing and celebrating that we are all inextricably connected to each other by a power greater than all of us, and that our connection to that power and to one another is grounded in love and compassion. Practicing spirituality brings a sense of perspective, meaning, and purpose to our lives.

—BRENE BROWN

I HAVE ALWAYS BELIEVED that there is something bigger than me "out there." I hold great respect for all faiths and believe that it is beautiful and sacred when someone is following a strong spiritual path. For me, this path has been shaken up several times. I have not followed an organized religion since attending a Presbyterian church as a child. When I went off to college, I began looking into different faiths and religions, attempting to find one that might fit with my beliefs. I kept thinking there might be one that I was particularly drawn to, but never quite felt at home with any of them. I do envision that there is an energetic force that connects all of life. I sometimes call it God and occasionally the Divine.

After my son died, I had a very confusing relationship with God. I felt I needed something to direct my anger at, and what better place than toward a God who I believed loves me unconditionally. I would vent, pray, ask questions, and seek answers to questions and enlightenment on matters that I knew I would never get the answer to. I couldn't understand WHY such horrible things were happening to me. I would pray to "whoever was listening out there," but felt that my trust in that listener was greatly shattered. I began to develop an overwhelming anxiety that more terrible things would continue to happen to me. After all, I was obviously not immune to disaster. I knew my faith was shaky. I even turned to sources I never would have before. I started reading books by various "experts" about the afterlife and spirituality. I remember reading some story about a woman who could communicate with spirits and who did "spiritual" readings. I don't quite remember what that entailed, but I was fascinated with the idea of being able to connect with something ethereal or trying to make contact with "the other side."

After both losses, I knew I had to find some sense of peace within myself. I had to calm the tumultuous mess of emotions that I felt on a daily basis. Even though I did not attend church, reading inspirational books about hope and persevering through life's struggles lent me support and gave me moments of peace within each day. There were many times when I needed to retreat from the noisy sounds of people or cars. Sometimes, though, the quiet was not always welcome because I would have difficulty with negative or fearful thoughts filling my mind. I gradually found that going for long walks was one of the safest ways for me to retreat into a quiet and meditative mode.

While I lived in my sister's neighborhood, I was able to follow a walking trail lined with trees next to a creek. I would push my daughter in her stroller under the leafy shade. Ella was too young to talk, so our time together was very peaceful and quiet as we absorbed the nature around us. I began observing the trees, small animals, and signs of life with a focus I had never used before. If I saw a rabbit, squirrel, bird, or turtle down near the creek, I would stop and watch it intently and even take joy in the simplicity of its existence. It was a gentle reminder that life was going on around me, but with much less drama and far fewer complications. I began to feel that nature itself was nurturing me, reminding me that life still offered beauty and calm, and that I was also made out of these elements. I began to look forward to these walks and even ventured out on days that were 90 degrees and humid! That is how much I craved this period of sanctuary. I always felt as if I had accomplished something at the end of my walks—a small feeling of peace, rejuvenation, and relief from the usually dark thoughts in my mind.

As I began seeking some sort of faith, belief, and trust in life again, I found comfort in the images of angels. I wanted to surround myself with gentle and uplifting imagery that would remind me that there were aspects of life that were greater than me and also out of my control. I remember visiting an art store in a cute little mountain town called Tryon, North Carolina, that was filled with unique folk art paintings, locally crafted mixed-media art, and handmade jewelry. I was instantly drawn to a pair of beautiful angels wearing blue dresses that were painted on two wooden panels. I envisioned them hanging on either side of my bed watching over me at night. I turned the panels over and saw that the angels were named Katie and Ella. Ella is my daughter's name, and her nanny at the time was Katy, who had been a saint to me in the early stages of my grief. She was gentle and kind with my baby girl and was someone I could trust to take care of Ella on the days when I could not get out of bed. Both of them were two of my earthly angels. That was a sure sign that I should purchase the folk art panels—immediately—and I have them hanging on my wall to this day.

If I had lost my belief in everything completely, I think I would have plummeted to a place of despair. I have gradually found more peace in my belief that there is another, more wonderful existence and mystery beyond this plane. I've also felt that, at times, Tookie or Brian has tried to contact me, or I've felt a presence that can't quite be explained. It's my own deep-rooted feeling that our souls never truly die and that life continues in some way. I know I need to have patience as my beliefs continue to evolve with my personal growth. As I've looked around at the things I *do* have in my life—a loving family, a healthy daughter, trustworthy friends, and life's basic necessities—I've gradually started to trust in life again, little by little. I think, "How could all of these other amazing things come into my life if there was not something larger than me looking out for my well-being?"

Dear Friend,

Whatever your belief system, or whatever you feel called to do regarding faith or spirituality, allow your spirit to guide you. You may deal with many questions or feelings of anger and disbelief in regard to the beliefs you held before your loss. Some people have a complete shift in their belief system after a loved one dies, and others find an even deeper connection within their faith. You have to do what feels right for you. Do not let anyone influence you otherwise. It is your mind, your heart, and your own internal wisdom that will lead you in the direction you need to go.

You might surprise yourself with where your thoughts

are taking you. Several women I've spoken with in my support groups have considered going to different spiritual healers, have spoken with mediums or psychics, or have withdrawn from their former beliefs. For others, their faith in God was questioned, but then strengthened, after their loved one died. It is not wrong to want to ask questions regarding life after death, or to struggle with your faith or trust in life. You may wish to talk to a spiritual counselor or share what you're feeling regarding your beliefs with someone you trust. Rebuilding trust in life again can take time after your world has been shattered. This is simply a part of your journey and personal growth. If you keep seeking, you will once again find your own personal truth and rediscover what beliefs you hold.

Love and Light,
Elizabeth B.

HIP CHICK WISDOM

"Our loved ones are with us, always. Open your eyes with your heart and you will feel them in everything you do."

—Katie E.

Me First (But Don't Forget the Baby)

This is what I need!

Breathe. Ask for what is needed. Practice courage.
Be gentle on yourself. Trust that it will be okay.

—KELLY RAE ROBERTS

learned early on when I was coping with my baby's death—and again after my husband died—that I had to be very specific about what I did or did not need from those around me. I used to be a shy person and often played the mediator in any situation involving conflict. As I was working through my grief process, however, I started to see that a new, bolder side of my personality was begging to come out. I could no longer walk a quiet or timid path through life. My path was suddenly filled with an inner fire and tenacity I never knew were within me. I became more courageously direct about every aspect of my life than I ever had before.

I started recognizing my need to be direct with people when I noticed that my family and friends were struggling in their attempts to help me. I knew they probably felt like fish out of water—not knowing how to tend to my emotional wounds—and so I believe it was helpful for them to hear me tell them things like "I need some water," "Could you please take that phone call for me?" or "I just need you to sit and listen to me right now." I was very candid with my thoughts and feelings. I had been broken open in an emotionally violent way and felt nearly every part of my soul was on display already. And I was coming to realize which aspects of my life I could and could not take on by myself.

For example, I remember sitting on the floor of my sister's upstairs landing at one point and going through a bunch of legal and financial papers—both aspects of my life that were way over my head. I couldn't make sense of what half the papers said, and as a result I was a bucket of emotions. I was overwhelmed with feelings of anger, anxiety, and helplessness. I had to simply say, "I can't handle all of this. It doesn't make any sense to me, can you please contact an adviser or I just might lose it!?" Jennifer got right on it and contacted someone who could help us. In her words, "As a caregiver, you never feel like you can do enough to help someone who is grieving. However, I think it's generally the simplest things that are helpful. It's also best not to ask what you can do to help; just tell the person that you're doing XYZ."

Forthright behavior has become a permanent part of who I am. I notice that I am not afraid to start conversations with new acquaintances, to share my opinions, or to express the true nature of my feelings no matter what the situation. This part of my emotional growth is the direct result of my grief journey. Because I put my thoughts and feelings out there on the line, I've also learned to fine-tune the way I approach people so I don't sound harsh or insensitive at times.

I now realize that developing my voice involved developing courage. I needed to have this strength in order to deal with the multiple facets of my life that had never been mine alone to handle before. I was a single mother, housekeeper, cook, and head of finances. Oh yes, and on top of it all, I was grieving. Did I need help? YES! Did

I need to directly ask for it at times? YES! I had to admit that I did not know everything and that in some areas I needed guidance. Yet, I could make the ultimate decisions about areas in my life. I could say "no thank you" to certain advice and could accept the things I truly needed. I noticed that as I gradually took on new duties I was taking care of myself, too, by becoming more assertive. By gradually taking on decision making and asking for help, I was not completely overwhelmed by every aspect of my life!

Dear Friend,

Sometimes it can be very difficult for those around us to understand what we truly need. Yet we who are grieving may think that people should be able to read our minds or come up with their own ideas of how to be helpful. This can put too much pressure on our friends and family, though. Unless they have been through a similar loss, they may not know the first thing about what to do. In the effort to save everyone extra hardship and frustration, you may just need to speak up sometimes. Most likely, your caregivers will appreciate your direction and resolve.

For some of you, being direct may not come naturally. It can take some practice, but just remember to listen to the truth that is within you. This will be your guide. Pay attention to that inner voice in your heart and mind—the one that lets you know when something doesn't feel right—and then communicate your needs clearly, whether in person, via email, or even in a handwritten note. You may even find this liberating.

Being direct is another way to take care of you. This is especially important if you've had to take on a lot of extra responsibility: overseeing finances, managing your home, or caring for children on your own. It is important to ask questions or admit that you need help with the things you've never had to do by yourself before. Asking family, friends, or professionals for their help or opinions can even be a way to empowerment. Each loss brings growth with it, and learning to handle new experiences and taking charge of your needs is part of the transformative process.

Love and Light,
Elizabeth B.

HIP CHICK WISDOM

"We're grieving, not running a race. We don't need cheering and words of encouragement from the sidelines, we need support."
—*Tiffany K.*

I come first? It's okay to be a *little* selfish?

Love yourself first, and everything else falls in line. You really have to love yourself to get anything done in this world.

—LUCILLE BALL

AS I MENTIONED IN the introduction, I'm the youngest of the three girls in my family, and I admit that I've always had the luxury of being a little spoiled. After Jennifer and Megan both left home, I was raised like an only child, and I always felt that my parents put my needs first. Later on, after I married Brian, I discovered my needs couldn't always be first. For instance, I no longer had complete say over where I was to live because we moved to where my husband's employer was located. Some of them were the last place I would have chosen to live! Eventually, however, I found myself back in the Midwest, in Missouri, where Brian could get a free education through his National Guard service.

I'm not saying that I gave up all my dreams for someone else, but I did realize that I had to be flexible in any decisions I made about my career and my own educational opportunities. I made a strong effort to make it worth my while wherever we lived, and I wound up attending graduate school at the University of Missouri at St. Louis, studying Community Counseling. But in general, my main focus had switched from "me" to "family."

After my losses, everything suddenly became about me again (which included my daughter, of course). What did "I" want to do with my life? Where did "I" want to live? What kind of care did "I" need? Making decisions on my own and not having to run them by anyone else was uncomfortable at first. And, strangely, I almost felt like a child again, wanting others to answer those big issues for me. But I gradually understood that it was about making choices that made "me" feel good and that made "me" feel happy. Although that "me" focus may sound selfish, it was critical to reclaiming my spirit and inner strength. I was suddenly the sole leader and needed to take the reins on how my immediate future was going to unfold. Making my first solo decision to move to Charlotte, North Carolina, with my daughter strengthened my belief that I was capable of making important choices for my own well-being as well as Ella's.

DECIDING WHAT'S NEXT

Here are some questions to ask yourself as you consider the future for yourself or for you and your child or children.

LIVING SITUATION

- What are the benefits of living where I am?

- What are the benefits of moving elsewhere?

- Where is my support system and how would it impact me to live close to them? If I am already living close to my support system, am I getting the help I need?

- What type of living environment do I want to create? How would I go about creating that space?

EDUCATION/CAREER

- Do I enjoy my current career or educational pursuit?

- Has my loss affected the way I feel about my current career path? If so, how?

- Would making a change in this area bring more joy and fulfillment into my life?

- What are my options when it comes to my education and career?

- What am I passionate about? If I want to make a change, what is holding me back? How might my life look different if I took a new path?

I began to realize that in order to function and maintain healthy relationships in my life, I had to make decisions based on what my own intuition and reasoning told me. I also began to notice that when I didn't take care of my own emotional, physical, and mental wellness first I was no good to myself, my daughter, or the other people around me. I had to be in control of my own destiny. I could not worry about what other people's expectations were for my life. I had been hurled into pits of fire and the depths of despair, and it was my choice how I chose to climb out of it and what I chose to make of my new life. I remember my sister Megan saying to me after my losses, "We don't care if you want to run off and join the circus at this point; we just want you to be happy!"

PRACTICAL RESOURCES TOOLBOX

LEGAL

National Organization of Estate Attorneys
(www.netplanning.com)

FINANCIAL

Social Security Office (www.ssa.gov)
Women's Institute for Financial Education (www.wife.org)
Financial Assistance/Grants for young widows
(lizlogelinfoundation.org and
tedlindemanoutreachfoundation.com)

HOUSING

DIY Home Improvement Information (www.doityourself.com)
U.S. Department of Housing and Urban Development
(www.hud.gov)
Habitat for Humanity (www.habitat.org)

CAREGIVERS

Babysitters, Nannies, Childcare & Senior Home Care (Care.com)

As I gradually began feeling stronger and more independent, I became more comfortable making decisions that were centered on my needs and wants. I liked getting to pick my first apartment because the energy of the space felt good to me. I enjoyed decorating my room in colors that were my favorites. I appreciated that I got to decide when I started my day and the routine that I created for myself. In the mornings, I'd sip my favorite coffee while making my daughter's breakfast; I'd take a midday walk, and then do my errands in the afternoon. If I didn't feel like answering the phone some days, I didn't. I would respond to the messages when I had the energy. I created a structure to my life that worked for me, and I didn't worry about what other people thought of it. It was about creating what worked for me in my particular situation.

Dear Friend,

It can be so easy to become overwhelmed with what you think you should or shouldn't be doing with your time. Yet, when you've experienced the loss of a family member who was so close, you need to remember that it is okay to be a little selfish about how you run your life. If you feel like you are bending over backward to make others—your children, your parents, your siblings, your friends—happy all the time, you are going to run out of fuel fast. It is okay to make your own decisions and to grieve on your own time.

Some of the choices you make might not always turn out to be the best ones, as you will see in the next section, but at least you are learning as you go. As long as you are doing things that resonate with "you," that is what is most important. Remember, the way each day unfolds starts with you. As I said earlier in this chapter, it is important to find your voice. Do not let yourself become any further depleted by ignoring signs that you need to be attentive to your own needs. In the long run, your children, family, and friends will thank you for *being a little selfish* and learning how to become centered and grounded again. You will be a much more pleasant person in general, and in turn you will have more to give back to others!

Love and Light,
Elizabeth B.

HIP CHICK WISDOM

"Death and loss can be a magnet for toxic people. It's okay to distance yourself from these negative influences, whether they're family, friends, in-laws, or coworkers, until you've had time to process your emotions. Don't feel guilty about it. You've been through enough. Then, once you've decided to move forward, don't let ANYONE hold you back."

—Faye H.

"Never be afraid to do the things you love in order to bring yourself healing. When my father died, someone made a comment that gave the impression it was wrong for me to 'already' be doing an activity that brought me peace and healing, my version of prayer/connecting with the spiritual. People will say things, and whether they think they are comforting you or processing death in their own way, may you find the inner strength to find yourself, your unique needs, and do what you must to heal by your own means no matter what anyone else says."
—Michelle Z.

I am Superwoman! Give it a rest, sister

When a woman becomes her own
best friend life is easier.
—DIANE VON FURSTENBERG

AS A WOMAN, I'VE always felt like I need to be everything to everyone. Need a shoulder to cry on? Here I am. Need a listening ear? Here I am. Need the bills paid? Check. Need supper cooked? Check. Baby's diaper changed? Check. Not that I've never had help with any of these things, but I think I speak for most women when I say we feel like we need to juggle a million roles in life, we should be responsible for these tasks, and we must make sure that they're done right! After all, no one does them better than I do anyway! Well, except for the cooking maybe.

I felt like I had to wear a Superwoman cape *before* my losses, so how on earth could I maintain my unearthly perfection (just kidding) *after* these devastations? Well, the answer is simple—I couldn't. I couldn't handle all of those things perfectly beforehand, so why stress myself out further and try to be great at everything while grieving? I'm not saying that I didn't put in the effort, but I recognized my limitations. One thing that often happens when we grieve is that we can become forgetful. In widow circles, this is often called having "widow brain." I could probably fill an entire book with all the things I messed up or did wrong.

One example that stands out was when I was going on my first trip after my husband's death. I was supposed to make sure that while I was gone everything would be set in place for my daughter, my apartment, and a pet fish that a friend had given to me. I accepted her gift even though I couldn't even keep plants alive, much less a fish, but I figured it might be nice to have another sign of life in my new apartment. Well, I managed to get the care needed for my daughter by leaving her with my sister. But I had forgotten to leave her the key to my apartment so she could get in to feed the fish! When I returned home, there he was, his limp (and smelly) body at the bottom of a fishbowl filled with murky water. I was sick to my stomach—both because of the smell and because of my inability to even nurture one of the easiest animals on the planet to care for.

There were also several times when I forgot to pay my bills. It was one of those tasks that honestly felt too hard to keep up with. I remember turning my water on one day without result. On my front door were several notices warning what would happen if I didn't pay the water bill (although, in fairness, I rarely used the front door!). I remember thinking, "This is ridiculous. I'll never let *that* happen again," only to have it happen two more times in the next few months. I think my electricity was shut off at one point too. I would get so overwhelmed by mail and other responsibilities that I would put them in a nice big pile on my dining room table and forget about them in the hope that some invisible friend might magically take care of them for me.

"Running late" was also becoming my middle name. Once I had gotten almost halfway to a therapy session when I realized that my gas tank was unbelievably low. I swear I was almost willing my car to "keep going!" Yet, when it started to make a sputtering noise, I knew I was not going to win and managed to pull into a gas station just in time. However, as I reached into my purse to get out my debit card, I realized I had left it on the counter at my sister's house! I was literally stuck. I didn't have a cent on me. So I wound up sobbing to Jennifer on my cell phone (such calls were second nature to me then) asking her to bring my debit card right away or I wasn't going to make my counseling appointment! Being a saint, she showed up in her van about fifteen minutes later and I made it to the last thirty minutes of my appointment. When I arrived, breathless, my counselor said, "Wow, I commend you for being so determined to get here!"

These are just a few examples of my failure to be responsible because of the cloud of grief I was under. I admit that when these incidents occurred, I got angry with myself and broke into tears at my inability to do anything right! Over time, however, I began to understand that these "crises" were a normal part of my readjustment. Life was going to go on regardless of my grief, and there were times when I was just going to fall behind. I had to begin thinking of myself as my own friend, or I would be forever frustrated. So I learned to be more forgiving of myself.

I still struggle with remembering things today and with getting certain things accomplished, but isn't that life? I finally had to give myself a mantra to repeat every day, reminding myself that I was human and would make mistakes, and there was no reason to shoulder all the responsibility alone. I didn't have to be Superwoman. It wasn't worth the extra stress!

Dear Friend,

Everything assumes a different intensity when you are feeling the pain of a loss. Be prepared. A minor annoyance that you might once have managed with a shrug now becomes a nuclear crisis! You are no doubt going to do things perfectly imperfectly. That is part of our path as humans. Forget about striving for perfection while dealing with grief! If you beat yourself up every time you forget something, have a breakdown, or don't do something correctly then you're going to end up very black and blue. I guarantee you won't want to look in the mirror! So be kinder and more patient with yourself.

You might feel like you are constantly struggling to keep up with life. The unfortunate reality is that life doesn't slow down for any of us, no matter what our trials. But in the chaos of daily life, it is important to learn to say, "I forgive myself." You may accidentally wear two different colored shoes, let your plants (or fish) die, or forget someone's birthday, but at the end of the day, you really *are* a "superwoman" in the sense that you are trying to do your best and striving to move forward with your life after a major loss. You should receive a gold medal for getting through each day no matter what it brings and then waking up and doing it all over again.

As time passes, and if you are working on your personal healing and self-acceptance, you will gradually notice that the "business" and distractions in your mind start to lessen. But remember that you need to think of yourself as your best friend; you need to love and forgive yourself when you slip up. Be careful not to create artificial expectations that put too much pressure on yourself. Just remember to view yourself and your humanness with a kind heart.

Love and Light,
Elizabeth B.

HIP CHICK WISDOM

"Do things at your own pace and on your own timeline. Don't be afraid to lie around all day in your PJs because it's all you have the energy for. Be kind to yourself and don't make harsh decisions too soon. Always remember that people love and care for you, even if they seem like they don't; they just don't always know how to act in response to your loss."

—Heather L.

Make sure the kids are all right

> If you aren't nurturing yourself, what
> kind of mother can you be, anyway?
> —SANDRA SCOFIELD

I'VE OFTEN HAD FRIENDS who don't have kids say to me, "I don't know how you manage to take care of a child when you're drowning in grief!" I just say to them, "I couldn't imagine *not* having my daughter while dealing with my losses." I've had the unfortunate experience of grieving both without a child in my arms and with a child in my arms. The situations are very different.

When my son died, I couldn't stand not having a child to care for. Although I was able to sleep for days on end if I wanted, life was too quiet. There was no one for me to take care of other than myself. Looking back, I can see now that being able to focus on myself allowed me a period of solitude in which personal growth could take place, which taught me the importance of self-nurturing. The importance of self-care has stuck with me since, and I believe it prepared me for the next losses I would face.

Because of my daughter, my second experience with loss was completely different. Even though, thanks to my family, I was able to get the rest I needed, I still felt my maternal responsibility and deep desire to be there for Ella as much as possible and to take an active part in her growth and development. After all, I hadn't been able to experience watching my son grow up; there was NO way I was going to miss my daughter's childhood because I was grieving.

In the first few weeks after my husband's death, because of the amount of shock I was in, I knew it was best for Ella to be with family members who could interact with her and make sure that all of her needs were met. But as the weeks went by, I gradually was able to become more involved again. I would hear her beautiful laughter in the next room while I was lying in bed in the morning, and it would call me out of my place of solitude to join her and my nieces while they played with each other. In a sense, Ella brought me back to life. She was the first person to make me smile again and brought a sense of purpose to my days.

Because I was almost chronically tired, and Jennifer had a full-time work-from-home job, I knew I was going to need to hire some help. It was something I was extremely grateful to be able to do. I had never sought out a nanny before, and I was very nervous leaving Ella with someone new. I barely felt comfortable leaving her with relatives, so it was another trust issue that I was going to have to deal with. After interviewing several nannies with my sister, I finally found a woman named Katy whom I felt comfortable with. She had two grown daughters and a third who was still in high school. She also had been a Montessori teacher, had a love of working with children, and possessed a kind and gentle personality, so she was more than qualified to care for my child. I had explained my history of loss to her so that she would understand why I was "the strange lady who slept late and stayed in her pajamas all day." Katy was very kind and understanding about my situation. I didn't feel judged by her in any way, so I knew she was a good fit.

I often struggled with feeling guilty about not spending enough time with Ella those first few months, but my friends and family kept reminding me that she was happy and getting the loving attention she needed. They assured me that, in the long run, I was being a better mother to her by taking care of myself. And I did find this to be true. As I was able to process my feelings, get the sleep my body needed, and attend counseling appointments, I gradually built up the strength to become more interactive and involved with her care.

When Ella was about ten months old, I began taking her to classes at The Little Gym, where she could play active games, learn acrobatic movement, and develop her motor skills, along with interacting with other toddlers her age. Those were moments of pure joy, getting to watch her laugh and have fun on the mini equipment. I wouldn't have been able to be as present with her had I not taken some time for myself. After she turned one, I even enrolled her in a Saturday art class as I eased into the reality of being a single mom. It actually turned into a great escape for me—to be surrounded by pretty, "pure" artwork that arose from children's imaginations. I was healed by their beauty, innocence, and creativity. The space was filled with natural light that enveloped you as you walked in. I think I looked forward to the art classes as much as Ella did!

I also felt empowered by putting a schedule together for the two of us, but I made sure it was within the limits of what I could handle. I didn't overcommit myself, yet these special learning activities with my daughter offered an incredible bonding experience and I could see and feel that I was a good mother despite the pain and grief I was coping with.

As my daughter grew older and her sweet yet stubborn personality emerged, there were plenty of moments when I was about to pull my hair out! I remember one time after we first moved into our apartment when I could not get her to stop crying about something. After trying unsuccessfully to calm her down, I eventually left the room. I started crying, too, because I couldn't handle the loud noise and stress. After taking time to compose myself, I was finally able to calm Ella down. I realized then—and now—how important it was for me to leave the room for a moment and take some deep breaths.

Raising a child is exhausting work without having to deal with the pain of grief as well. I learned to pace myself in order to be fully present for my daughter's needs and to respond to her in a calm and collected way.

Dear Friend,

It is important to remember to take care of yourself in the midst of trying to take care of your child or children. Being a mother is emotionally and physically draining, even without grief. So, when you add in the grief, it is like running a double marathon each day. Don't forget to slow down and take time for yourself. If you have the ability to hire a nanny or find a friend or relative who can help watch your daughter or son—if only one or two times a week—I suggest that you do it!

If you run yourself ragged taking care of only your child's or children's needs, then you end up losing patience, strength, understanding, and the ability to handle even small situations. You will reach your breaking point eventually.

You do not need to feel guilty, either, about not being the perfect mother while dealing with your grief. Women already do that to ourselves even when we are not grieving! If the children are old enough to be coping with the loss, along with you, you may want to find a grief support group for them to join. (Even though you may be there for them in every way you can, you cannot be responsible for every aspect of their personal healing. Trying to become your child's full-time counselor is not another thing you need to add to your full plate of responsibilities.)

SUPPORT FOR GRIEVING CHILDREN

There are many great resources out there for children who have lost a family member or friend. By contacting them, you can both get the additional support you need so that you can cope as a family. You can be strong for your child or children and provide amazing support; just don't forget to pay attention to your own feelings in the process.

Here's a short list of some of the resources available nationwide:

- The Dougy Center: The National Center for Grieving Children and Families (www.dougy.org)

- Kindermourn (www.kindermourn.org)

- National Alliance for Grieving Children (www.childrengrieve.org)

Being a mother while coping with grief is about finding balance. You want to get to a place where you are working on your own healing process and also be able to spend quality time with your child or children. This is another area of your life where you should not be afraid to ask for help. If you feel that you are getting burned out trying to parent each day (even if you have a spouse or partner who is trying to help) call in reinforcements! This will allow you the opportunity to retreat to a room to cry if you've been holding back tears for hours on end, do an activity that helps you relieve stress, or simply take a breather to give attention to your own thoughts and feelings. You will end up stronger (and less crazy) in the long run if you allow yourself what I call "sanity breaks." Your children will appreciate a calm, well-adjusted mommy too!

Love and Light,
Elizabeth B.

"Mothering while grieving should involve being understanding and keeping a gentle attitude toward yourself as you work to balance your own needs and your child's. You become stronger by remaining aware of your own well-being, which in turn makes you a stronger person for your child or children."

—Elizabeth B.

The New Normal . . .
Baby Steps, Please

Okay, this is socially awkward.
Am I *that* abnormal?

> The psyches and souls of women also have
> their own cycles and seasons of doing and
> solitude, running and staying, being involved and
> being removed, questing and resting, creating
> and incubating, being of the world and
> returning to the soul-place.
>
> —CLARISSA PINKOLA ESTES

would consider myself a pretty average-looking person. I've got two arms, two legs, and long blonde hair. But occasionally when someone hears about my losses, I get this look (you might know this look well) as though I'm an alien with two heads. I've heard from some of my widow friends that they've even had people take a step away from them after hearing about their losses, as if their unfortunate circumstances could possibly be contagious. Now, I'm not saying this is true with everyone who knows my story. Quite the opposite. If I'm in the right environment, and someone else has also experienced the loss of a loved one, it brings about the most amazing form of connection with that person. There is a level of understanding that you both feel comfortable with, which in itself is healing.

In the first year of my grief, there were times when I felt like hiding my personal story of loss and other times when I wanted to wear a sign on my body that read "Be nice to me, I'm grieving," or "Don't tick me off; I've already got the world on my shoulders," or maybe even "BEWARE—don't upset the widow!" I needed a variety of signs that I could switch out depending on my daily mood.

Some of the most poignant times for me were when I took my daughter to mother-baby classes that were full of other moms whose husbands were alive. It was especially hard to hear them talk, complain, or joke about their husbands, and almost painful when they would occasionally drag the men to the activities. I had to steer clear of those conversations. If I heard anyone utter one word of complaint about her husband, I'd tune her out.

I have friends who have gotten irate in those circumstances. My dear widow friend Tiffany, for instance, managed a shoe store. Just two months after her husband's death, she was waiting on a customer who wouldn't stop complaining about her husband—how selfish and cheap he was, how he never wanted her to spend any money. Finally, after struggling to fit a shoe on the woman's foot, Tiffany couldn't stand it any more and shouted, "At least your husband's alive!" She fled to the storage room while her assistant calmed the woman down, explained that Tiffany had just lost her husband, and finished the sale. Now, this may not be the ideal way to handle the situation, but I can easily understand why Tiffany reacted the way she did and can even imagine myself doing the same thing.

"Normal" activities, such as going to the park, shopping at the grocery store, or doing things with my baby girl, were challenging for me for quite some time. It seemed as if everyone else was going about a normal, wonderful life and completely oblivious to the fact that my loved ones were gone forever. Why hadn't the world stopped? Didn't they know how important those two people were in my life? What was wrong with everybody? Couldn't they show some respect and mourn along with me? It took some time for me to realize that many other people were probably hurting too. Some people just hide it better than others.

Dear Friend,

Journeying through grief is one of the most "normal human" experiences you can have. Nevertheless, all too frequently the heartbroken seem to feel alienated by society. Unfortunately in our culture, we are taught to hold our feelings in. If someone asks us, "How are you doing today?" the expected answer is, "I'm okay." But what if you aren't okay? You obviously don't want to go into a monologue of why you're not okay, but sometimes you feel as if you're going to explode if you can't "tell off" that well-meaning person for even daring to ask you such a thing in the first place!

There were times when my insides felt so raw I was surprised that people couldn't see my pain written all over my face. We Americans are taught to say "I'm fine" no matter what disaster or tragedy is affecting our lives. Of course, it is the polite way to respond, but it's another reminder that things are severely wrong in your world. I just want to assure you that whatever roller coaster of emotions you are riding—whether they are feelings of anger, sadness, despair, anxiety, or even small moments of peace—this is all normal! Grief can make us feel crazy; don't be afraid if you feel the need to express yourself, as long as it doesn't cause you personal harm or harm to others. Even though at times you may want to punch some insensitive person in the face, please try to refrain.

Love and Light,
Elizabeth B.

HIP CHICK WISDOM

"In my opinion, some of the worst words of encouragement have been 'Everything happens for a reason,' or 'This, too, shall pass,' or 'I know how you feel,' or 'They're in a better place,' or 'Things will be okay.' These phrases always make me want to promptly introduce someone to my fist."

—*Tiffany K.*

Can I hurry this up, please!?

> Never compare your journey with someone else's.
> Your journey is your journey, not a competition.
>
> —AUTHOR UNKNOWN

I CAN'T TELL YOU how many times I've thought, " I am SO sick of feeling this way! Will this pain and heaviness ever end? This is torture!" I spent the majority of the first six weeks in bed after the loss of my son and then again after the loss of my late husband. I *know* how hard it is to find that drive to keep moving. As I've shared with you in earlier chapters, you absolutely need to allow yourself time to sit with the pain, but there is also a point when you can't let it hold you down as if it were an elephant sitting on your chest.

And with this in mind, please be gentle with yourself. I rejoined the world gradually. First it was just taking short walks outside, then it was having a family member drive me to counseling appointments, and eventually I was able to walk into stores full of people. But every time I ventured out, I usually had at least my sister or a close friend with me. This may not be the case for everyone as far as reentering the community, but I found it calming to keep my support system close by.

It was at least a good six months before I started to find some bearings, when I could really begin to live more on my own. I was so lucky to have a supportive sister who welcomed me into her house, but after several months, I began to feel that I was imposing on her family's life. She never said I was imposing, but I knew I eventually had to begin creating a life for myself, and my daughter, again. So

I began by getting an apartment near my sister's house, about five minutes away. I would spend part of the morning or afternoon at my apartment, but when it started to get dark (which was often one of my loneliest times), I would take Ella back to my sister's home, where we would stay the night. It was the feeling of security that I needed at that time.

I know this arrangement isn't possible for everyone, but it might not hurt to have company during those lonely times of the day or night, whether it's an hour-long phone conversation with someone you can confide in or a best friend camped out on your couch overnight. As the months passed, I was able to begin sleeping at my own place without feeling such high anxiety or sadness. I developed a routine of putting my daughter to bed, turning on some of the "light" TV programs that I mentioned earlier, making a special nighttime snack out of anything that included chocolate, and cozying up on the couch with a big blanket. On nights when I couldn't sleep, I would spend time writing, reading, or surfing the Internet for resources on grief.

As I was coming out of the fog of shock after the first year, my emotions were unpredictable. In fact, I continue to be unpredictable to this day. It's not as extreme as it was during the first or second year, but there are times when I have moments of high anxiety or feel so overwhelmed that I break into tears. I realized as early as the end of my first year of grieving that I had to leave myself room to be flexible. I scheduled only activities I felt comfortable with, such as being around just one or two trusted people at a time, and I did not over-commit to things.

For instance, the first Thanksgiving after Brian's death, I was a mess. It had only been three months since he had died, and getting through a holiday was the last thing on the planet that I wanted to do. To prevent my breaking down into tears during the meal, I asked that everyone make it as casual as possible and to keep the conversation light and to a minimum. They respected this wish, and we proceeded to have a quiet Thanksgiving dinner. (This is only one of many things my family did for me.)

I did end up having one breakdown that day, which did not surprise me. My nieces, my stepdaughter Lily (from my late husband's first marriage), and Ella all gathered for a family photo in front of the fireplace. They wore matching outfits and hairstyles and looked as cute as can be. My daughter was ten months old, so she was propped in one of the older girls' laps. Just as the picture was about to be taken Ella started squirming and ended up falling face forward and landing flat on her head. I went running toward her trying to cushion her fall. My family tried to reassure me that she had a hard head and was going to be just fine, but I had been deeply shaken by watching her fall. I ran upstairs and into a closet. I stayed in there and sobbed for several minutes.

Eventually my sisters, with patience and tactfulness, coaxed me out of my hiding place. But I assure you if you ever end up crying in a closet you are very normal. I was eager to stop feeling so out of control with grief and wanted to able to handle myself in a "normal" way. I was frustrated that I couldn't enjoy a family gathering. It was still hard to not see myself as some kind of freak for a while, but after speaking with other people in my support group about their own behaviors, I eventually didn't feel so bad.

Dear Friend,

The intense roller coaster of emotions will gradually lessen over time. But there is no time frame for the grieving process, and it will not be rushed, no matter how fast you'd like to "get over it." The reality is that there is no getting over it; you can only walk through it.

There is such a thing as getting stuck in your grief, however, which is very detrimental to your health and well-being. This usually takes the form of depression. Given that you have been through a tremendous and transformative loss, you are absolutely going to feel depressed. But it is important to recognize when you have been detached from life for too long. The fact is you are still alive, and I can only imagine that your loved one would want you to go on living. I highly doubt they would have said to you, "When or if I die before you, I want you to spend the rest of your life sitting on a couch staring at the wall. Please fulfill this important task for me." Believe me, I know that sometimes it is hard to get up . . . sometimes it just feels impossible. You may have to take baby steps out of your depressed state. I know I did.

Taking baby steps can involve some creativity. (A full list of Creative Hip Chick Ideas is included at the end of this book, by the way.) Creativity doesn't only refer to art; it can apply to all areas of your life. For instance, you may need to creatively come up with an idea for getting out of bed in the morning. You might consider setting a small goal for yourself, such as, "I'm going to try a new flavor of coffee this morning," or "I'm going to call that new lady I met in my support group and invite her to lunch." Another one might be, "I'm going to go look for a scrapbook album today so that I can start working on a memory book." Even if you get out of bed, yet don't complete the exact task you set for yourself, that's okay! You have at least begun taking the steps. You may even find that you feel drawn to do a different activity than you originally planned.

One thing I have often heard from people who are grieving is that they feel pressured and rushed by others to hurry up and get through their grief. You may feel like you are being forced to take part in activities that you don't feel ready for. Remember to listen to yourself. If it makes your blood boil or you feel close to tears just thinking about the event, don't do it. People who haven't been to the depths of pain that you are experiencing can't possibly know how insanely hard it is for you to put on a happy face and attend a party, go on a beach trip, celebrate a birthday or holiday, or even just run regular errands. I've found that it's best to stick with those people who are the most understanding about what has happened in your life and who give you the room to process and work through your emotions.

Love and Light,
Elizabeth B.

HIP CHICK WISDOM

"Live your life for yourself but also by the lessons you have learned through love. We love so deeply that it is not possible to heal overnight. But one day you will smile, laugh, and live again. Your loved one wants this for you."
—Katie E.

"We may feel defeated when pain from grief that we believe to be complete reappears. Instead, this is testimony to our growth. We are ready to process a piece that we could not have processed before, and this leads us to even more healing and self-realization."
—Carol P.

Did I really just buy *all those shoes*?!

> She stood in the storm, and when the wind did not blow her away, she adjusted her sails.
>
> —ELIZABETH EDWARDS

SEVERAL MONTHS AFTER I moved to Charlotte, my girlfriend (and former shopping partner) Malerie came to visit me. I had been in the process of redesigning the space I lived in with Ella, trying to make it more "mine." I wanted to redefine the place I was living in just as I was redefining myself and my place in the world.

I shared with Malerie that I hadn't done much for myself in a while and I was feeling the need to replace some of my older clothes and personal items that I had grown tired of or didn't want to keep any longer. She proceeded to take me on a shopping trip to Target, and we somehow ended up in the shoe section. Imagine that! As we walked down the aisles, every time I pointed out a pair of shoes that I was interested in, she'd grab my size off the shelf and toss them in the cart. A part of me wanted to protest, but a part of me also felt a slight sense of liberation. I was certainly shopping within my budget, but this was the first time I had splurged on anything in a long time. I don't even remember how many pairs of shoes I left with, or what other articles of clothing I purchased, but it did help to get out of my apartment and see some new scenery—especially with such a trusted friend.

This was the start of allowing myself to get creative with my surroundings. I've always been very affected by what I wear and what is in the environment around me. I discovered that it felt good to get rid of (or at least store away) some of the items from what I considered my "past life." I wanted to experience a sense of rejuvenation and therefore gave myself permission to revamp some of my wardrobe as well as my new apartment. I think it gave me the feeling of moving forward, even though I was only partially feeling ready for that. I remember thinking, "I want to feel better, and if buying those pairs of shoes is going to help lift my spirits temporarily, then that is okay!" I knew it wasn't going to solve anything on a deeper level, but I did feel that I deserved to spoil myself a little. A widow friend of mine, Katie, said that in the first few months into her grief, she was drawn to the color pink. She began purchasing pink shirts, pink nail polish, and various other pink articles of clothing. She had never been drawn to it before, but something about the color resonated with her. She later learned through a friend of hers that pink represented calm feelings, relaxation, and contentment—all things she was craving in her life.

As I began to beautify my new space, I wanted to create as relaxing an atmosphere as possible. I purchased a new comforter, some new wall hangings, a cozy rug, and some original artwork from a friend of mine. I made sure to keep the lighting soft and kept some scented candles near. It was about creating an environment that I felt safe in and soothed by.

As I continued with my grief therapy, I gradually met other women who were allowing themselves a little "shop therapy" as well. I have one dear widow friend who bought herself a luxury vehicle that she had been lusting after for some time. She had always been a hard worker, and there was a phenomenal deal on the car, but as she was wrestling with making the decision whether or not to buy it, I gave her the added encouragement to go for it! After all, we only live once, and if she had the means and ability to buy it, then more power to her. And now when we go out for some girl time, I don't mind the added bonus of getting picked up in her pretty ride!

Dear Friend,

It is okay to treat yourself (within budget of course) when you are in the grieving process. Maybe it's time for you to buy those fancy heels you've been admiring. It is also important to allow yourself the opportunity to redefine the space in which you live, which can bring a renewed sense of energy. It doesn't have to be the next "Extreme Home Makeover," but allow yourself the freedom to transform your surroundings a little with pieces of art. It may be refreshing to simply rearrange the furniture in your house or get some new scented oils or candles that inspire peace and calmness.

Sometimes after a loved one's death, you can develop the feeling that things are very stagnant. But you may have a hard time changing the space around you if you lived there with your loved one. It may seem as if you are letting other pieces of them go if you change your physical surroundings or you change the way you used to look or dress when they were alive. But the reality is that all your memories are held in your heart and mind, and even if things change in the way you decorate or how you look, it will not erase any of those memories. You do not have to live in a museum, frozen in time, or feel that you don't deserve something that you might enjoy. After all, you are still alive and it is perfectly healthy to do things that make you feel good.

Love and Light,
Elizabeth B.

HIP CHICK WISDOM

"When your mind starts wandering toward the thoughts of 'If only I . . .' or 'Why didn't I . . . ,' immediately redirect your brain to 'I am so grateful we . . .' and 'I am so grateful for . . .' Follow that with stating out loud, 'I am so grateful to have had the time I had with my loved one.'"
—Maria S.

Discover the Revamped (And Quite Fascinating) You!

Still more losses to deal with? How much can I handle?

> I've broken open many times.
> But I am not broken. I'm just alive.
> —KELLY RAE ROBERTS

With the loss of both my son and my husband came many more (smaller) losses. It's sort of like that saying, "When it rains, it pours." With Brian's death I also lost my identity as a wife and all future plans that I'd had, such as moving to Washington, D.C., to take a job he had been planning on after his deployment; traveling to Bora Bora and Greece; and having another child. I gave up a home that I felt comfortable in. It was small and cozy with lots of natural light. It was only one story and easy to take care of. I even gave up my dog because I didn't feel that I could adequately care for him on top of my other responsibilities. I had lost the support of a partner, and most of all, I had lost trust in life. I felt like life kept letting me down, and so I began to feel depressed.

One of my widow friends shared that she personally felt her sense of "home" had disappeared when her husband died. As she put it, "My husband was my home no matter where we were. When he left, that was gone. All sense of security, comfort, well-being, and hope were smaller losses to deal with. I also lost loved ones who did not know what to do or say. I lost relationships that I thought were solid and important. This was a very difficult way to learn that they were neither. For the first time in ten years, I was making decisions that were only about me. I still thought and spoke of 'us,' but I'm no longer part of a team."

In my depression, I also felt a loss of self-esteem and confidence. I was overwhelmed by the mountain of loss I was feeling! I remember that right after I had gotten everything arranged in my apartment I was struck by the amount of downsizing that had just taken place in my life. At one time, I had lived in a three-bedroom house with a huge backyard. My home had always been filled with movement and voices and laughter. But after my relocation, I found myself in a small, quiet apartment with empty white walls. Most of my possessions were in storage or stacked in boxes in my tiny garage. It wasn't just a feeling of emptiness; it was a barrenness that cut straight into my soul. It was a visible reminder of how my life, once so full and busy, had suddenly come to a standstill. All these changes I had undergone were just additional losses that I had to readjust to.

I kept asking, "Why do I have to keep giving things up in my life? Why do I have to keep letting go all the time?" I didn't understand why I kept losing the things I had always dreamed of having—the things I had wanted the most. Ever since I had been a little girl, I'd known I wanted to have a family some day. Yet, I felt like it kept slipping through my fingers. Was it really so much to ask for? It felt like a wicked joke was being played on me.

One hot North Carolina summer day, I left my daughter with my sister so I could run some errands. When I returned home from grocery shopping and pulled into my garage, I could feel the tears welling up. I thought of how I was going to be walking into a completely empty house with no one (not even my dog) to greet me or to help with the groceries—just overwhelming silence and loneliness. The only thing that felt slightly welcoming when I walked in my back door was the air-conditioning. After dragging in numerous plastic bags and cursing all the way to the kitchen, I knew I was on the verge of losing it. I threw the heavy bags on the floor, collapsed next to them, and started sobbing. They were angry tears. I think I even kicked the wall. I had the intense desire to break something, but nothing was close enough to grab, and I didn't have the energy to reach for anything. I'm sure my neighbors above had long since thought of me as the crazy lady downstairs, but I couldn't have cared less.

Dear Friend,

Losing a loved one is a major hurdle in life. You have lost an important presence in your life. And with that you've also lost conversations, familiarity, and companionship. If you were a caregiver to your loved one, you might have grown used to a certain routine and suddenly you have a lot of extra time on your hands that you don't know what to do with. If you lost your partner, you undoubtedly had a flow or pattern worked out that helped you move through each day with some predictability. And, to make things worse, you may be experiencing other unexpected losses as well. There may be a loss of stability, a loss of financial security, a loss of routine, a job loss/change, or a loss of a home or a change in environment.

These additional losses will catch you off guard some days. They sometimes come in the form of moments when you hear a song that reminds you of your loved one or when you're approaching an event or experience that would have involved him or her. It is okay to release your feelings when you feel the waves coming. It's all part of the process of having to let go of your relationship with your loved one as you once knew it. And remember, letting go is not the same thing as forgetting! It is important to give yourself permission to continue a connection, or a different form of relationship, with your loved one in the way that you remember him or her through stories and memories. In this sense, your loved one continues to impact your life and "live on" in the world by the way you honor them or share their spirit with others.

Love and Light,
Elizabeth B.

HIP CHICK WISDOM

"I went through a major bout of depression after my husband passed, and I never thought I would be the same. One thing I learned from that experience is that we hold on to the pain/depression because it's the only emotion we can feel that is as intense and pure

as what we just lost. I know it's hard, but some day you'll be able to move forward on your own terms. I am still moving forward, and every day is a challenge, but I know that he would not want me to stop living our dreams."

—DeLanie T.W.

This is making me feel old

They always prided themselves on looking youthful. "Forty's the new thirty," they'd joke. Until heartbreak and grief enter your life, and then forty's the new one hundred.

—MELINA MARCHETTA

THERE IS NO QUESTION that grieving is exhausting on all levels. It has had the ability to make me feel old (and wise) beyond my years. After both of my losses, I felt like an eighty-year-old living in a twenty-seven-year-old's body. I knew I had experienced deaths that most people either don't experience until they are much older or sometimes never experience! I would look at myself in the mirror and think, "I look familiar, but I don't look quite like myself anymore." I suppose the grief was transforming me inside, and it was affecting how I saw myself physically.

Sometimes I feel like I've lost all my emotional innocence. There were times very early in my grief when I felt like I should pull on a granny sweater and stare out the window of a nursing home. I thought, "How am I ever going to find a morsel of youthful energy again?" I was entirely depleted and felt I could no longer relate to other women my age, particularly friends I had been close to for a long time. I was still able to maintain a sisterly bond with most of my longtime friends, however, and my experiences also opened up opportunities to make a new circle of soulful friends who had been through a similar type of loss.

As I've had more time in which to heal, I've been able to access my feeling of youthfulness again. I can still dress up and go out and feel attractive, but it took some time to get back to that place. When one of my girlfriends came to visit, for example, we decided to go dancing. I had studied dance in college and had always found dancing to be a way for me to de-stress and relieve tension. I thought it might be a good way to remember a part of myself that I felt I had been losing.

It was a very strange feeling to get dressed up, but it also felt good. I remember looking in the mirror and thinking, "I actually don't look as old as I feel!" As we entered the dance club that night, I remember feeling very out of place as we swerved among moving bodies and laughing people. It was another reminder that life was still going on around me, despite what I had been through. My goal was to avoid making conversation with anyone and to simply focus on the music. I didn't know how I would handle even the simplest questions, such as "How are you?" or "What do you do here in Charlotte?" I certainly wasn't going to answer those questions with, "Well, I'm honestly not that great because I've just lost my husband and my infant son" or "I live in my sister's bonus room and this is my first night out in months."

I did end up getting involved in a conversation with my friend and a group of people at one point, but I kept the conversation as low-key as possible. My answers were short and didn't reveal much about my past. At that point, I was not ready to go to those deep places inside myself. I wanted to attempt to be in the moment and enjoy the distraction of the loud, pulsating music in the background. Overall, I think it had been good for me to get out and do something that woke my spirit up a little. I did feel a sense of new energy after participating in something that I had once loved to do.

It took me several months to realize that I was not mentally old; I was simply "wiser." I eventually came to embrace this wisdom rather than feel anger at the events that had brought me this deeper knowledge about life. I learned that I had to achieve a balance between holding this wisdom and allowing myself to let go a little, to be impulsive, and to experience new things. I can now say that I'm grateful for the knowledge I can pass on to my children. I'm able to teach them what truly matters in life, and to not take things for granted. This is something I remind myself of every day.

Dear Friend,

You may feel as if you've aged several years in your grief. It is natural to feel that you have grown old overnight due to the consistent aching in your heart and the trauma of what you've been through. You may have once been full of energy and motivation and felt ready to take on the world. Yet, losing a loved one depletes the mind, body, and soul.

I know it can be tempting to curl up in a ball and wait for life to pass you by. But the fact is, you are still here, and it won't do any good to waste away on the couch or to throw in the towel and think, "Well, now that my loved one is gone, life is completely over." The reality is that your life is not over; it is changed, and painfully so. But it is not time to call it a day just yet.

Gaining wisdom through our losses in life is part of the spirit's development. It is important to acknowledge and honor it as part of your growth. (This is part of our phi-losophy at The Respite, www.TheRespite.org.) The wisdom you have gained is something you can pass on to friends or family members who find themselves enduring grief—for there surely will be those. Once you have walked down the grief path, what you have gained on your journey may turn into invaluable advice for someone else. Remember, grief is an experience that touches everyone at some point. Even if you've lost a parent or grandparent through the nat-ural cycle of life, it is never something you can truly feel prepared for or "old" enough to experience. Life passes by before we know it.

So if you're starting to feel depleted or older than your years, I recommend getting out with a friend or family member. Take a walk several days a week. Try to find a new route each time. Join a yoga or meditation class. Plan a night out with some friends. You are still here on this earth to experience things with the time that you have, and I imag-ine that your loved one would want you to live your life to the fullest.

Love and Light,
Elizabeth B.

HIP CHICK WISDOM

"By expressing our feelings, we open the door to hope by connecting to our hearts."

—Carol P.

Identity crisis: Who am I now?

> It's not your job to like me—it's mine.
>
> —BYRON KATIE

AFTER LOSING MY BABY and my husband, I felt very confused about who I was. After all, I had come to know myself as a wife and mother with specific plans for her future. I had been making a new home and enjoying new motherhood with Ella. Then, suddenly, my whole life changed. I was even unsure of my capabilities as a mother to my daughter. After moving to my sister's house, I was without a home, my life was packed away in boxes, and all the plans that had been guiding my life had evaporated.

I felt like I had no direction. I had worked as a teacher after graduating from college, and then I was pursuing my master's degree in counseling, but after the death of my son and the birth of my daughter, my priorities had changed to being a stay-at-home mom. Then Brian died, and suddenly I realized I didn't know what I was going to do with myself or where I belonged or even where I should live. I had thought that I was beginning life as a new mother after my daughter was born and now, in my grief, even that seemed to be an overwhelming task.

However, I began to recognize that there was a part of me that was stronger than I ever could have imagined. I didn't know how I was still standing. I surprised myself. I was waking up to the fact that I was in charge of my own life and that it was my choice whether to sink or float. It was strange because there was a part of me that felt like a fragile child in my grief, and then there was this other side that felt like a powerful warrior—fighting my way through the pain in order to survive. Consequently, there were many times when I looked in the mirror and thought, "Who is this person?"

At about the same time, I began to realize how much I was comparing my life experience to that of people who had not lost a child or a husband. I felt the pressure to fit in with the world around me. But I soon became aware that I wasn't the only person who didn't have a picture-perfect life. There was a lot of suffering and loss going on near me; it was just not obvious from outward appearances. As I struggled to find a new path for myself, I knew that I needed to reconnect with my spirit. This led me to seek out self-help books, attend group meetings, start an exercise routine, and create new friendships with women in my support group. I even tried some new things I thought I would never do, such as become a beauty consultant!

On one of my first major outings after moving into my apartment, I attended a cultural festival with my friend Michelle. There were several different vendors there, including one that sold skincare products, and I decided to register at their booth for a free facial. This was about eight months after I had moved to Charlotte, and I was really beginning to feel restless. I wanted to find something I could do that would allow me to have flexibility and create my own schedule. I needed to be my own boss because I didn't want to be accountable to anyone else. If I was having a particularly bad day, I needed the ability to withdraw and not potentially get fired. I wear my heart on my sleeve, so when I was having a particularly bad day or moment, it was always obvious—painfully so to my family and friends.

After the skincare demonstration, my girlfriend suggested I become an independent sales consultant. I was skeptical at first (especially since beauty treatments were not one of my top priorities), but I gradually began to think, why not? I wasn't doing anything else with my time other than watching my daughter, and I knew I needed to start thinking about earning an income, so I signed on the following week. As I became more involved with my new business, I began to meet a lot of really amazing and empowered women. There always seemed to be laughter and good times with this group of ladies. It was great being around women who knew how to joke and make fun of themselves. I was finding that through my time with them, more than anything else, I was regaining a sense of humor.

I also learned how to properly take care of my skin, and I began to put more of an effort into taking care of myself as a whole, both on the outside and the inside. I began to enjoy feeling like a woman again, and even took time to dress up in heels when I'd go to give customers facials. I was also reminded of the skills I had: my attention to detail, my strength in communicating with others, and my joy in connecting with almost anyone. Overall, spending time with my fellow consultants and clients was quite therapeutic. I began to feel stronger within myself, and after several months I was starting to grow more confident. I could see that I still had the necessary tools to function in the world. It is a cliché, but I discovered that work was therapeutic and, more important, that I had something to give to others.

Dear Friend,

I'm not recommending that you run out and become a beauty consultant, but do something that entices you to reach out and contribute to the world. Sometimes it comes down to trying something new or something you may have least expected. This is a surprising aspect of the grief journey. You will find yourself faced with alternatives you might never have considered before. Don't run away from them. You may come across new people or new opportunities that allow you to see new sides of yourself, or rekindle elements of your inner being that you've lost touch with.

It can be intimidating to feel as if you have to get to know yourself all over again and to figure out a new sense of purpose or a new way of approaching your life. There are large and small ways of experiencing this shift. If your loss did not impact your overall lifestyle, you might have experienced a shift in your perception of the meaning of life. Perhaps your eyes have opened to how fragile our existence is, and you are trying to integrate this new awareness into the way you choose to spend your time. Each loss gives us the opportunity to view things differently. This may change your perceptions of yourself or of specific aspects of your life.

With anything that takes time, you need to be patient with yourself. You may find yourself thinking, "I never felt or acted this way before my loved one died," or "Who have I become now?" (For a further discussion about this issue, see the section called "Did I really just say that?" in chapter 8.) It may take some soul searching, connecting with new resources, or talking about your confusion with someone you trust. You may decide to set a new goal for yourself. You may be surprised as you shift into a more evolved version of the person you already were!

Here are some tips for positive change that you might find helpful as you discover the new Hip Chick within you:

- Begin a new exercise routine.
- Adopt new, healthy eating habits.
- Find a new "look" by playing with your wardrobe and hairstyle.
- Volunteer at a shelter, a school, or an organization that you feel passionate about.

- Create new friendships.
- Read inspirational stories.
- Travel to a place you've always wanted to go.

Love and Light,
Elizabeth B.

HIP CHICK WISDOM

"Thinking of just me is difficult, but necessary, and eventually the decisions I made brought me comfort. And hopefully they are helping me to build a life full of love, support, and—one day—happiness."

—Katie E.

Would You Like More Salt for That Wound?

Happy holidays?
I'll take a rain check, thank you

Become a possibilitarian.

—KELLY RAE ROBERTS

I had the unfortunate experience of having both the nightmare **before** Christmas and the nightmare **after** Christmas. My son died in January 2008, following what had otherwise been a pretty magical and exciting Christmas that Brian and I spent anticipating his birth. Then, after my husband died in August 2009, I had to face a parade of holidays, birthdays, and anniversaries that followed all in a row. September was his birthday month; October is my birthday month; then came Thanksgiving, Christmas, and New Year's; Ella's birthday is in the beginning of January; the anniversary of Tookie's death is at the end of January. How on earth did I do it?

By the time February rolled around, it was as if I could finally take a deep breath again. During that first year, each holiday and anniversary found me in the doldrums—crying, yelling, sleeping, and complaining. Those who chose to stick around me were either very brave, very foolish, or masochistic! They deserve a serious pat on the back and some cupcakes with sprinkles. I was a MESS.

I spent my twenty-eighth birthday—just two months after Brian's death—with my dear friend Michelle. We went to my favorite sweets store near my sister's house: they made gourmet cupcakes! I bought half a dozen in several different flavors. I wanted to keep things low key, so Michelle and I went back to my sister's and sat on the floor of my bedroom and lit a candle on one of the cupcakes. I made a wish that my life would somehow get better, and that I would find hope and happiness again. I spoke the words out loud and Michelle listened to me try to process the fact that I was turning a year older while my son and my husband were now buried. It was another one of those moments when time seemed to stand still, or perhaps I was lost in time. I do remember smiling that night, though, thinking about how they must be watching over me. I could really feel their presence that day.

It's slightly easier to get through something like Halloween. I bought a spider costume for Ella and made a quick walk around the neighborhood. Everyone is in costumes so what you look like doesn't matter. Thanksgiving, however, was the first big stressful family holiday I had to endure. (You might recall that in "Can I hurry this up, please!?" in chapter 4 I described the parameters I set for the occasion to make sure I could get through it without dissolving.) Thanksgiving requires conversation and relatives and a certain amount of stressful preparations. It's like a dress rehearsal for Christmas. I made my appearance at the table, but I was going through the motions like a robot. My body was there, but my mind wasn't.

When I reached Christmas, I made it all about Ella, who was just about to turn one. I knew I had to put on a brave face for her and let her enjoy her very first Christmas. My family did a great job of making sure she was spoiled, and I just sort of sat back and watched things unfold around me. I was so grateful for her smiling face, because that's probably the only thing that got me through. To be honest, apart from watching Ella open her presents, that day is a blur: wrapping paper all over the floor, piles of food I couldn't eat, endless and meaningless chatter I didn't want to hear . . . A part of me had quite simply checked out, which is not unusual throughout the first year of shock. I think I spent the entire day in my pajamas and didn't move far from the couch. I also spent a lot of time staring out the window.

I didn't want presents that first Christmas. Instead, I asked everyone to give a donation to charity in honor of a loved one. Perhaps I didn't want to feel that anything was superficial, and giving to others in greater need than I was seemed more important. I found a program that helped widows and orphans in Africa, so I focused on giving to that organization, and it made the gift-giving easier. I found that reaching out to help others seemed to bring some purpose to my life—and it had been quite some time since I had felt any purpose. It gave me something to feel good about and also reminded me that there were others suffering throughout the world who didn't have half of the physical comforts I did. It helped put some things in perspective. Here I was with a loving family around me, a cozy warm house, comfortable clothes, and food to enjoy, while there were women out there suffering the same pain as me who didn't even know where their next meal would come from or how they would care for their children. Holding on to that knowledge throughout the holiday season reminded me that I DID have things to be grateful for.

Things were a little easier during the second Christmas celebration after Brian was killed. I felt more involved in putting up and decorating the tree. Because I had already been through it once before, I suppose I wasn't feeling as raw emotionally. And this has been the case with most holidays as time passes. The intensity of the pain wears off, and there is more room in my heart for new memories. As I've grown more accustomed to handling holidays and other special occasions, I've learned to not be so worried about what everyone else does. It's truly about what works for me.

Dear Friend,

There is way too much pressure surrounding the holiday season at the end of each calendar year. We are encouraged to go into debt buying lots of presents, throwing big parties, getting together with our extended family, and indulging ourselves in joy and laughter. Well, that isn't the reality for everyone, and the idea of a jolly holiday is like rubbing salt in the wound when our loved one isn't there. Do not pressure yourself to live up to a holiday card's cheerful musings or a holiday movie special!

There are a few ways you can approach the Thanksgiving, Christmas or Hanukkah, and New Year's holidays: you can either try to make them like they were before your loss, try something entirely different, or combine old traditions along with creating new ones. If you try too hard to make holidays, birthdays, or anniversaries exactly like they were before your loved one died, you're likely setting yourself up for a rough time emotionally. Things aren't like they were before, and no amount of effort will change that.

There are many women in my support groups, for instance, who have completely changed their holiday plans and traditions since their loved one died. One replaced the huge family Thanksgiving dinner with a quiet meal with a couple of friends. Rather than have the traditional family Christmas gathering, one took off on a cruise with her friends. Another chose to dispense with her elaborate Christmas decorations and let her neighbors put up a simple Christmas tree for her. Such changes give you more room in which to grieve in the way that you need to if you don't get too set on one way of doing things. If you're the type of person who likes to always be busy, you might even find comfort in planning something elaborate because it provides you with a distraction.

There are also many incredible ways you can bring your loved one's presence into the day's activities. You may wish to include them in a prayer at the table, light a candle for them, or tell warm, affectionate stories about a time you shared together when they were alive. You might also feel compelled to make a donation in their name to celebrate an occasion. Some of my family members donate to a children's hospital every year in my son's name for my birthday, at Christmas, or on the anniversary of his death. There is no right or wrong way to move through the holidays. It's about what works for you. Honor your grief. You may find a completely new way of handling celebratory occasions by starting new traditions, or you may feel more comfortable sticking to old ones. Either way, you will know what feels right.

Here are some tips for surviving the holidays and other special occasions throughout the year as an emerging Hip Chick:

- Volunteer to work with a charity.
- Take a trip.
- Go out to eat with friends on the holiday.
- Get together with someone who is without family or friends on the holiday.

- Attend a holiday concert; music lifts the spirit.
- Try not to sit home alone—at least not all the time.
- Make some comfort food with a friend or loved one.
- Look up some ideas for new traditions or rituals and try them.
- Make a donation to a cause in honor of your loved one.

Love and Light,
Elizabeth B.

HIP CHICK WISDOM

"Even though holidays and special occasions can be difficult, they can also be used to remember the good. Honor your loved one by including their memory. Make their favorite dish; continue to do what made them love the holiday. Keep their memory alive."

—Diane S.

The Other Side of Grief (Yes, There *Is* Another Side!)

Embrace your story; it's made you stronger

> Just when the caterpillar thought
> the world was over, it became a butterfly.
> —AUTHOR UNKNOWN

It took me quite some time to embrace my personal story of loss. I'm not saying that I accepted my losses as being "okay," but I began to accept the reality that this was my life story and it was shaping me into a stronger person. Through speaking with my counselor, I learned that I didn't need to run from my story or feel shame in it. I didn't need to feel uncomfortable that I wasn't the typical twentysomething woman. But I did not get to this point without some kicking and screaming! I BEGGED life to let my pain be just the "normal" headaches that we experience as women: having a bad hair day, forgetting where I put my car keys, or quieting kids who were yelling too loud. But I had to realize that this was MY path. I could not control the losses that happened to me, but I could choose whether to demean the power of those experiences or honor the ways that they transformed me. (We teach about honoring the transformative power of grief at The Respite and in The Model of Heart-Centered Grief at www.TheRespite.org.)

For instance, I beat myself up unmercifully with the thought that I should have been able to save my son. After all, I was his mother and my job was to protect him. However, after speaking repeatedly with both the ob-gyn and the midwife who had been present at Tookie's birth, it was made very clear to me that nothing would have changed the outcome. It was a tragedy that no one was responsible for, and as badly as I wanted to continue blaming myself, I had to stop causing myself more pain and suffering. I could not go back in time and change the circumstances. I had to learn to come to peace with that. Don't get me wrong, there are still plenty of times when I think "what if," but I don't allow myself to become tortured over what will never be. Otherwise, I would be condemning myself to a life of misery. I had to accept what had occurred in my life and move forward from a place of strength.

One aspect that particularly helped bring about this inner strength after Brian's death was the knowledge that I needed to be strong in order to re-create a life I would feel good about living and would positively impact my daughter. I began to realize that there was something sacred about the suffering I had experienced. It was opening up opportunities for me to help others in the world who were also hurting. I had always known I wanted to do something extremely impactful with my time here on earth, yet I had been floating around in the breeze before I lost Tookie and Brian, unable to find my purpose. Now, my mission had become clear!

But in order to fulfill my goal of helping others, I first had to embrace my story and to truly absorb the wisdom my experiences held for me—if I listened and learned. Because I had been so intimately exposed to the reality of my own mortality, I adopted the "go big or go home" mentality. I thought, Since my days here are numbered I don't have much time to waste, so I'd better get moving on any dreams now! This has led me to pursue a couple of endeavors (which I will reveal in the next chapter) that have me steamrolling forward like a freight train. I admit I've gained the ability to be fierce, and I don't accept "no" very easily if there is something I want to accomplish!

If I were to write a card to my grief, it would say, "Grief, even though I have a complex and painful relationship with you that has broken me open to my core, I want to thank you for giving me a more fearless spirit, for teaching me to focus on the present, for motivating me to go after my dreams without question, and for giving me immense gratitude for the love and beauty that I have had and continue to have in my life!" I do **not** like the whole package that these lessons came in, but after all the tears I've shed, I have openly and even joyously accepted the trickle of amazing gifts that have gradually come throughout my healing process. I now wear my grief journey with dignity—accompanied by three- or four-inch heels, depending on my mood. Some days I even feel like a warrior goddess!

Dear Friend,

Learning to embrace your story and your grief journey is not an easy task, but it is an essential part of moving forward. Your loss is part of what has molded and shaped you into the person you now are, and the person you will become as you continue to open your heart to life. It is important not to view your grief as an enemy but as a wise ally that will nurture, guide, and comfort you out of the depths of pain and despair. Just as grieving pulls you into the depths of sorrow, it can also be the force that pulls you out. It may be helpful at certain points throughout your grief journey to ask yourself these questions: "What is my grief teaching me?" "Where is it guiding me?" "What am I being called to create?"

Embracing your journey is a form of acceptance. It is coming into the full reality of what you have endured and honoring the depth of what you've experienced. Despite all the pain and suffering in the world, your experience is still unique and therefore should be honored. This means you have something to offer others through your story. It is a gift you hold within yourself. You have the power over what you do with this gift. You may greatly impact one other woman and empower her to lead a more meaningful life, or you may impact thousands of people. Just remember that your story is sacred. The journey you have walked is a powerful one; treat it with the utmost respect.

You may notice a newfound sense of strength as the weight of your pain gradually begins to lessen over time. This should be embraced, too, as it is a sign that you are moving forward on your grief journey (not forgetting or letting go!). Your experience of loss is forever a profound part of you and has made you wiser, stronger, and even more beautiful because it's transformed you . . . into a warrior goddess.

Love and Light,
Elizabeth B.

"Sometimes out of great tragedy come amazing things. You can use your grief to change the world."

—Diane S.

Wow, is that resilient woman really me?

Grief is not a disorder, a disease, or sign of weakness. It is an emotional, physical, and spiritual necessity, the price you pay for love. The only cure for grief is to grieve.

—EARL GROLLMAN

IT WAS AT LEAST seven or eight months before I was once again able to function after each of my losses. The emotional pain was still constant, but I felt as though I had a little more room in my head to think about other things in my life so I could begin thinking about new goals. Now this did not by any means mean I was feeling "great," but I was starting to take steps to move forward . . . such as having the strength to go on a trip, spending more quality time with my daughter, and getting out of the house a bit more. As one friend told me right after I lost Brian, the pain never completely goes away, you just sort of get used to it. That sounded pretty depressing, but

I've actually found it to be true in that the pain gradually becomes more manageable and not so overwhelming. This is a part of our natural resilience as human beings.

Dear Friend,

As a woman who has been through two significant losses, I want to say clearly to you yes, the pain is unimaginable and yes, you will get through it. Some people deal with the pain in unhealthy ways such as through substance abuse, but I am here to advocate a healthy way of coping with the pain and loss. Even though at first it may completely consume you, that indescribable feeling gradually becomes lighter over time, as long as you allow yourself to process it. If you try to escape from or numb the pain, you are just setting yourself up to end up back at square one. The only true way to move forward is "through." Does it stink? YES. But if you don't take time to listen to your feelings and let them out in healthy ways—with a counselor, support group, or trusted family and friends, for example—then you are basically a ticking time bomb.

As I've mentioned several places earlier in this book, I highly recommend finding some mode of support. We all handle grief in our own way, but one thing we all have in common is that holding on to grief gets us nowhere.

Seeking professional support or help from a support group does not mean we are weak—in fact, it takes strength and courage to ask for help. And, in the end, it will make us stronger. It's not always easy to express our feelings, and

I've been to some support groups where some of the attendees choose to sit in silence, and that's okay. It is still therapeutic to listen to others tell their stories. So stop making excuses if you feel stuck and haven't sought genuine help yet. It won't hurt more than the pain you already feel. I can promise you that. Seeking professional help was the way I found my way out of the darkness, so I am a strong advocate of seeking out healing resources. It's the reason I'm able to share my healing path with others today.

Love and Light,
Elizabeth B.

HIP CHICK WISDOM

"The choice of conscious healing is a wonderful dance that we do throughout life. We face the reality of loss and, in so doing, engage all our losses. When we find the pain of the reality too much to bear, we dance in and out, sinking into the abyss of our grief and healing as we are able. We move from numbness to anguish to pain. We move through longing, sadness, missing, and gratitude, again and again."
—Carol P.

Was that me laughing
just now & having fun?

> We cannot selectively numb emotions;
> when we numb the painful emotions, we also
> numb the positive emotions.
>
> —BRENE BROWN

I HONESTLY COULD NOT remember the first time I laughed after experiencing the loss of both my son and my husband, so I had to ask my sister! She told me that it happened the day after I got back from traveling to Germany (where I sat by my husband's side as he was taken off life support). I was in bed watching some family videos on a tiny camera with my friends, Diane and Michelle, and both of my sisters. I imagine I must have been deliriously tired and was at one of those points where I felt so terrible that my only options were to laugh or cry. Then again, I had "my girls" by my side, all of whom could get to the heart of me any day. If anyone could revive a spark of life in my spirit at a time like that, they could.

The next time I recall laughing was when I connected with my new young widow friends, Erica and Tiffany, a couple of months after I moved with Ella to my sister's home in Charlotte.

I met Erica in a widows-widowers support group. She was about a year into her grieving process, her husband having died in a motorcycle accident. What I immediately noticed in speaking with her was that she was actually able to poke fun at herself for the "silly" things she did while going through her grief. She also would skip work whenever necessary because of her emotional upheaval (with no apologies!), and she showed off a little bit of her "spunky" side by dyeing a section of her hair pink. Erica inspired me because she was LIVING. She didn't know what the future held (she's happily remarried now), but when she'd come over while I was in the middle of a meltdown, lying amid wads of Kleenex all over my bed, she could make me do a full-on belly laugh! There was nothing like laughing with another woman who had been through a similar experience of loss!

Erica taught children with developmental disabilities and would poke fun at herself for being a thirty-year-old woman who wore fun-colored "kid's" tennis shoes similar to the style her students wore and how she was lucky to have a job with flexible work hours so that she could take time off on her "bad days," also known as "sick days." This is "widow humor."

I met Tiffany through an online widows forum. The website features a bio section where you can explain the circumstances of your loss, and when I read Tiffany's, I instantly thought, I have to know this woman! (She had lost her husband, an ex-Special Forces soldier, while he was contracting in Afghanistan.) I sent Tiffany a message, and we hit it off right away! She was living in Massachusetts at the time, but we found out that her older sister actually lived right down the street from my sister's house in Charlotte! We knew we were destined to connect, and eventually Tiffany moved to North Carolina.

Let's just say that Tiffany is a rather outspoken individual—and even that may be an understatement. (Do you recall the story in chapter 4 "The New Normal . . . Baby Steps, Please" about the shoe store manager who shouted at a customer? That was Tiffany!) She's one of those people who will go straight to the core of something but manages to inject humor into it with the timing of a comedic genius. For instance, if I was being hard on myself for being forgetful, she would say something like, "I'm lucky I even remembered my own name today, so you're doing better than I am!" I met her on several different topic areas within the widow's forum, one of which was talking about our current love life situations. Tiffany began writing about how she missed the intimacy she'd had with her husband and came up with the idea of a "widow's care basket." She named several "unmentionable intimate items" for the care basket that would basically assist a woman who was feeling lonely, which I thought was a pretty clever idea. After a couple of weeks, however, I noticed that Tiffany hadn't visited the forum. She then sent me an email explaining that she had been bullied off the site by several widows who had been angered and offended by her seeming insensitivity to their feelings. I felt bad that she had been treated in such a way simply for being open-minded and honest. She never intended to be offensive. But my first reaction was to laugh! I mean, who gets kicked off a widow's forum??

My first major trip after losing Tookie and Brian began with a girls' vacation to Jamaica for four days. This included Tiffany and one of my late husband's best friends, Lisa, and her sister Christina. I couldn't imagine a better combination of strong women to spend my time with, healing, laughing, and temporarily escaping. The only part of the trip that was challenging for me was leaving my daughter for several days. It was the first time I had been away from Ella for that long since she was born. But I knew my family had things under control and that she was in good hands. I knew I needed the time to focus solely on myself and work through the waves of emotions that I was always struggling to not capsize from.

Let's just say that when a group of women travels anywhere together, or gets together in general, there is ALWAYS a ton of laughter! I think that was the most healing part of the trip for me. Every night at dinner we wound up laughing over stories of bad past dating experiences, various travel adventures, funny memories, and comparing the unevenness of our sunburns. Of course, there were times during the day when I lay on the beach in a hammock, listening to the waves, and letting the tears flow down from beneath my sun-glasses. But I couldn't imagine a more perfect location for an emotional release. We specifically chose an all-inclusive resort that likely wouldn't be full of couples. Because who wants to look at that when you're still grieving your spouse? A lot of the population at the resort seemed to be groups attending family reunions or young people that had the traveling bug. So aside from the occasional headache from late nights dancing and one pretty bad sunburn, I'd say I felt like I was right where I needed to be at that time. I came back feeling a sense of rejuvenation and more strength to take on the world in front of me.

It did feel strange after each of my losses to laugh again for the first time. Often a feeling of guilt crept up and whispered in my ear, "How on earth can you even *think* about laughing at a time like this! Your loved ones have died and left the planet for good!" Yet somehow there was a counteractive voice in the back of my mind that would say, "But they would *want* me to be happy and smiling." This was a battle I fought within myself for several months after burying each of my loved ones. I knew, though, that it was unrealistic to say, "I'm never going to laugh or smile again as long as I live!" Unless I was planning on living in a hole for the rest of my life, it just wasn't humanly possible.

I eventually learned to embrace laughter as a welcome RELEASE from the heaviness in my heart. I believe I've already cried enough for twenty years' worth of my life. There will always be more tears to come, too, but whoever said "laughter is the best medicine" couldn't have been wiser. It creates a greater sense of peace within. After all, if we are so serious about every aspect of life we could end up turning cold and rigid. There is an appropriate time and place for it, but I always welcome the giggles when they start—when I see something hilarious on TV or read a funny story. I perceive laughter as another way to relax, rejuvenate, and recover from all of those heavy feelings that build up over time! Humor has become my best friend.

Dear Friend,

Never feel afraid or ashamed to laugh when the moment comes about. Even though you swear in the beginning that it will never be possible to do so again, a funny or endearing moment will come along. You may find yourself trying to fight it because it may feel wrong to you. Yet, what if it had been you who died? Would you want your loved ones to never laugh or feel joy again? I imagine that you would want them to feel happiness and peace whenever possible—even through their grief.

It helped me, especially in the early stages of grief, to remind myself that my loved ones would want to see me enjoying moments again. Also, I didn't feel that I could fully honor their lives by resorting to a permanent attitude of doom and gloom. It wouldn't be doing justice to their spirits: the bright, wonderful person I believe my son would have been; the full-of-life, kind, and determined person that Brian was. So consider the personality your loved one had and how much he or she loved you. Perhaps your special someone is the one responsible for some of the moments or events that make you laugh as you recall memories. Living life involves learning to enjoy it again, and it WILL be possible to let joy in as you travel your creative grief path. Who knows, you might even find yourself a "Tiffany" out there if you don't already have one!

Love and Light,
Elizabeth B.

"After my loss, I immediately turned to my best girlfriends. The only thing I needed to hear at that time was 'you will be okay.' Fortunately, I was able to hear that from one of my friends and then more as they learned about what happened. It's true . . . I was going to be okay. Reach out to friends when grief hits you. Ask for what you need to hear. The words will bring peace to your soul."

—Cindy B.

Yes, you're allowed to love again

> You are imperfect, you are wired for struggle, but you are worthy of love and belonging.
>
> —BRENE BROWN

GRIEF HAS HAD A way of stomping on, tearing apart, and even mutilating my heart. I used to think, "Can this organ ever be put back together? Will it ever feel love without pain again? How is my heart going to remain open after these tragedies? Won't it be easier for me to simply shut down and numb myself from feeling anything?"

When I'm speaking of love, I'm not talking strictly about romantic love. I mean love for all the people in my life and love for life in general! The simple fact is that I don't feel alive without feeling love. I had to choose whether I wanted to move forward with a broken and bleeding heart or take the risk of letting it love and feel loved again. Since I'm a risk taker by nature, I chose the latter.

In many ways, I've felt love in a more profound way now than I ever did before losing Tookie and Brian. I truly understand the depth of love I have for the people who stood by me through the worst of my pain and held my hand as I've walked my grief journey. When I felt like I was homeless after my husband died, my sister offered me a place to stay. When I believed that I was alone after becoming a widow, I found a community of women ready to embrace me. Those were amazing acts of love that I will never forget. As the anger surrounding my losses has gradually dissipated, there has been more room in my heart to let love exist. I've been given what I need in each moment in order not only to survive but also to thrive. After all, I realistically only have "the moment" to live in anyway. Giving and receiving love is a way of nurturing myself and seizing those moments.

Personal relationships have always been very important to me, and even in my darkest moments of despair, I knew deep down that I'd somehow find love again. I am a hopeless romantic, and my late husband knew this too. He used to jokingly say that if he died overseas (because of his dangerous job) I had only three days to grieve and after that I'd better move on and not waste time finding someone new to love! I remember protesting that it was ridiculous of him to even say that, but now I look back and smile at that statement. It was a testament to the fact that he wanted me to move forward and be happy again (although I'm sure he was not serious about the "three days").

Dating was never a world I wanted to reenter, yet there was no other choice but to date if I wanted to meet someone new and, hopefully, find love again. So I joined an online dating site and bravely checkmarked the box that revealed I was a "widow." I was actually curious to see what sort of prospects my widow status would bring. Surprisingly, it didn't scare men away as I had originally envisioned it would. After all, my widowhood instantly showed that I had been through a very emotional experience, and emotions are often something men shy away from. (At least that's what I've seen!)

The road to love is certainly never easy for most people, so I felt that it would be an added challenge as a widow. I gradually realized, however, that the only real difference in dating before being a widow and after was my level of experience with a relationship and knowing what I was looking for. Most of the men I went out with were quite sensitive and respectful of my past, although I did sense of a lot of curiosity from some of them about how I handled my loss—and about why I didn't "look" like a widow. I halfheartedly accepted dinner invitations from a materialistic guy who cared mostly about the car he owned and his visions of wealth. Then I went out with a nice guy who was super-talkative and more of a "friend" type. I also dated a thirty-year-old man who claimed he was ready to settle down, but really just wanted to party. And those are just a few examples! Every date ended with feelings of disappointment and dismay that I was once again in the dating pool. There were certainly nights when I cried myself to sleep.

A time finally did come, though, when I met a new man, Tim, who happened to be tall, dark, and handsome (which I didn't mind at all) and also ex-military. I swear that wasn't on purpose! I remember thinking, "Really, God? You're giving me another one of these crazy living-on-the-edge guys who like death-defying scenarios and major risk taking? Okay, so I guess I'm a risk taker as well, but really?!" When I first went to meet Tim, I was slightly nervous, but I had also come to a point in my personal evolution where I felt pretty comfortable with myself. As I pulled up in my car at the meeting spot we had agreed on, I thought, "Well, if he likes me he likes me; if he doesn't, oh well—it's his loss."

Tim greeted me with a kind smile and gave me a hug, which I admit surprised me a little. He is a big, strong "manly" man (an ex-mixed martial arts fighter and army sniper) so I wasn't expecting to see this gentle side of him so quickly. But there was an instant ease that kicked in right after we began talking. It was like being with a person I'd already known for a while. After sharing stories and laughing for about four or five hours, I told him I needed to pick up my daughter and he asked right away when he could see me again. I knew he was hooked! I think it was after only our second time hanging out together that he held my hand and asked if I'd like to pursue a relationship with him. He looked at me with his clear blue eyes (which he knows get me every time) and in the end I couldn't resist his charms.

As our relationship progressed, I decided to open my heart to the potential of what could be. And aside from some ups and downs on the way to creating a blended family (Tim has two wonderful, sweet children), we took the plunge and began a new life together as a married couple. Even though it was scary opening my heart (because of the fear of loss), I realized that it was possible to feel that kind of love and vulnerability again—and even that butterfly feeling in my stomach. I was aware that a new love would not heal all my past wounds (that is too much to place on another person), but it made me aware of just how much my heart was willing and able to love. Just how much I wanted to devote myself to this new man and our new path together. The way that my heart has been wounded, yet continues to deeply love, still amazes me! I suppose my heart is the most resilient part of who I am.

It has been a great learning experience for both my husband and me. I knew I would need to be with a man who was comfortable with himself, who respected my past and the way it has shaped me, and who could handle my occasional meltdowns and moments of anxiety. So there is a lot of navigating new waters. And I admit that in the beginning I felt awkward bringing up something about my late husband (my son is an easier topic) because it can be awkward even talking about an ex, let alone a partner who died. But as time passes, the reality of my past, and my ability to be in the present and look toward the future, continues to become more comfortable and "normal." As I see my husband accept and truly love who I am, despite my flaws, and vice versa, I appreciate the wisdom I have gained through my grief experience. Grieving has helped me become a stronger, wiser person in my marriage. I'm also grateful that my husband reflects my strength back to me. He once told me, "You're the strongest woman that I know."

I remember the first time I received a card from Tim after we were married. I believe it was for my birthday. He always makes sure to write a personal message in every card, and in this one he wrote about what an amazing wife I was and how lucky he was to have me. It was one of those moments where it really clicked in my mind that a new chapter had begun. I was proud of myself for truly living in spite of my fears—for opening my heart again and allowing love in, even knowing the risks that inevitably come with that territory. After all, my heart and spirit deserve to be loved, and that is a truth I hold dear.

I also remember hearing about some comments another woman made after she learned that I'd started to date again. These comments weren't said to me directly, but nonetheless, they implied that I must not have respected my husband or spent enough time grieving. This in my mind was absurd. I never did anything that I didn't feel ready to do in my own time (as should all grieving women), and there was never a day when I wasn't working through my grief at my own pace. It was hard to not feel offended by that woman's remarks, to not feel that I was being harshly judged. I admit that it really upset me.

But then I had to look at the truth of my situation, and I reminded myself that only I could determine what was right and wrong for my own life. This woman was merely projecting her own inner conflict on to me. I had to realize that I was dealing with someone ignorant of my experience. She had no right to criticize my actions when she had no idea about what I was dealing with. Despite my level of annoyance, I decided to take the higher road and vent about it with my close circle of support. It helped to discuss my feelings with those who truly understood my story and would support my decisions without judgment.

Dear Friend,

You deserve to love and be loved no matter what. Even though the pain of your loss may temporarily dampen your heart or force it closed, the natural inclination of your heart will gradually be to open again. This might take time. But remember to hold those closest to you. It can be healing to remind family or friends how much you love them. That even though your loss may have taken a large piece out of your heart, you are still infinitely grateful for the love surrounding you. It is important that you hear these words from them as well. Love is essential to your heart's wholeness. You may find yourself clinging to your loved ones like never before because you know how quickly people can be taken away.

If you are a widow or have lost a partner, know that it is okay to love again. Your loved one would not want you to be alone forever. Love will be found at your own pace. There is no particular time frame in which you have to wait after your loss, although I do recommend getting through the first year to at least allow the shock to wear off and to give you time to relearn who you are and what your new needs or hopes are. You may want to start dating before getting through the first year, and that is okay too. You have to do what feels right to YOU. Other people may have their opinions on this topic, but ultimately you are in charge of your decisions. Remember, there is no right or wrong way to do things. Listen to your heart, and you will know what you feel ready for.

Love and Light,
Elizabeth B.

HIP CHICK WISDOM

"Learning to live again wholeheartedly includes letting love flow freely in and out of your heart."
—Elizabeth B.

Telling Your Story, Sharing the Grief (You're Not Alone After All)

I'd rather not JUST survive

> Your beautifully messy complicated story matters. Tell it.
> —KELLY RAE ROBERTS

When I first heard the concept that there were gifts, and even HOPE, to be found through the grieving process, I'll admit I was hesitant to believe it. My counselor is the one who introduced me to this profound idea, and because she had never led me astray throughout our counseling process, I thought, "There must be some truth to this, and I'm going to figure it out! Where's the hope? Where's the joy? Just point me in the direction of where I'll find those feelings and I'll be there in less than a split second!"

I didn't realize throughout my healing process that I was, in essence, applying The Model of Heart-Centered Grief co-created by Mandy Eppley, MA, LPC, and Chris Saâde. (Learn more about their approach at www.TheRespite.org.) I was simply embracing new ideas and reframing the way I viewed certain aspects of life as they were put forth by my therapist. She would challenge me with positive viewpoints and give me gentle nudges as I fought my way through the depths of darkness and began envisioning a life in which I could hold my grief yet also allow joy in. I began reaching for life and new experiences instead of just trying to "make it" day in and day out. Although this process happened gradually, it also moved at a pace that quite surprises me to this day. The strength of my will to live and thrive and create new memories is something I am quite proud of.

The essence of the heart-centered grief model is embracing and honoring the lessons of our grief and transforming them into messages of hope, guidance, and growth. There are great gifts to be found by "mining" our grief and going into the trenches. If we allow our grief to transform us and teach us about ourselves, then we are able to take our new wisdom and use it as a means to give back to the world. This is a very empowering model, and I stand as a living example of someone who has greatly benefited from its teachings. (To learn more about heart-centered grief or to purchase the educational DVD series visit www.TheRespite.org.) This is not always an easy task, but I learned to be aware of my own small triumphs amid the sorrow and pain. What I viewed as taking a huge step in my recovery might not have seemed that big to anyone else. For example, some days I would be so proud of myself for getting to the gym or taking my daughter outside for a walk. Then, incrementally, those actions moved me toward becoming more social, going out more and meeting new people, and as a result, getting to know and respect myself in a new way.

I began to realize how much more appreciation I have for life on a daily basis. And I looked around at the incredible people who have come into my life since I lost Tookie and Brian, and I know that I never would have met or crossed paths with them had it not been for my grief journey. I would not have found the purpose I now have in life had I not experienced the loss of a child and a spouse. I don't have a doubt in my mind what my goal is each day: to help others who are suffering from loss. I'm not saying that the loss of my loved ones was an even exchange for discovering my purpose, but the way I dealt with my grief resulted in new blessings.

It has been satisfying to know that with what I have learned through my own pain and suffering, I am able, in some small way, to help others through the grief process. And I've realized that fulfilling my life's purpose involves sharing my story with honor and conviction. I am happy to speak of my experiences in the hope that other individuals who have gone through something similar may be touched to the point of believing in hope and seeking happiness again. The ability to do this brings a great amount of peace and healing to my own heart.

GIFTS I'VE DISCOVERED THROUGH GRIEVING

- Forming a circle of wonderful friends, leaders, and mentors
- Enjoying soulful business partners
- Being able to create an environment that brings me peace and comfort

- Discovering wisdom and joy that have transformed me into a more inwardly beautiful person
- Cherishing the "little" things even more
- Discovering the freedom I have to create and design my own life
- Having a closer relationship with myself and my loved ones
- Taking risks and becoming bolder

Through sharing my story and experiences I've realized that I'm not alone in this world. The extent of suffering in every corner of the globe is unimaginable. EVERY PERSON on this planet experiences heartache and a deep loss at some point. And everyone handles her or his grief differently. But the knowledge that emotional pain is a human experience, just as joy and happiness are, brings me a lot of comfort.

Another gift I've received is the opportunity to meet and witness other amazingly strong and beautiful people who have done incredible things with their grief as well. This type of beauty is all around us. I am moved to tears when I read an inspirational story or listen to a soulful speaker who is sharing a message of hope and joy after a personal loss. Since losing my baby and my husband, I have surrounded myself with positive-minded people who constantly keep me on the right track. They allow me to be in the reality of the heaviness of what I've experienced while also keeping me on the path of hope and inspiration—reminding me I can't hold the depth of my grief without embracing "the other side."

Dear Friend,

Surround yourself with inspiration. It happens to be all around us. Learn from the incredible role models in today's world who have gone through intense loss and hardship yet risen up to bring hope to others. You see them in the media (the good stories anyway), in books, and even in some of the people you meet. (I consider these people to be our modern-day heroes.) There are also wonderful quotes and sayings that can bring a little daily dose of wisdom and encouragement to your life as well. Use one of these messages as a screensaver on your computer; my coworker Cindy chose "Stay on the path" for her own encouragement. Or display one or more of them next to a mirror or any spot in your home that you walk past on a regular basis. There may be days when you don't believe in what these messages say, or you want to resist the wisdom, but these mental reminders will eventually become second nature in your train of thoughts. I have hung some wall plaques with uplifting messages next to my full-length mirror and above the light switch in my bedroom. This way, when I'm getting ready every morning, these positive reminders are some of the last things I see before walking out the door to face the day.

Consider asking yourself these questions: "Do I want to live each day simply surviving, or do I want to thrive in my life?" "What do I want to do with the time that I have left?" "Where can I receive some words of inspiration or wisdom?" I'm not saying it's possible to avoid all negativity, but try to protect yourself from outside doom and gloom to the best of your capabilities. For instance, this may involve not listening to the daily news, or setting up boundaries around certain people in your life who may not have a healthy or positive mindset. If you find yourself slipping, call someone who can help lift you up again, or reach for a book (such as this one) on finding hope and inspiration. You might be amazed at how many resources are out there.

Love and Light,
Elizabeth B.

 **HIP CHICK WISDOM**

"Trust leads to peace."

—*Patricia R.*

Creativity came calling!

I hope you will go out and let stories happen to you, and that you will work them, water them with your blood and tears and your laughter till they bloom, till you yourself burst into bloom.
—CLARISSA PINKOLA ESTÉS

I KNEW THAT DESPITE my broken heart, I did not want to live a life where I was "just existing." A deep part of me wanted to rejoin the world and do something meaningful with my life. After losing my son, I considered creating a group for mothers who had lost a baby. We moved from Missouri to Virginia not long after my son died, however, and I knew very few people. And then I quickly became pregnant and did not have the energy to create a new group from scratch.

After I was widowed, though, my desire to form a support group became my prime motivation and focus. Only six weeks after Brian's death, I began formulating an idea for a young widows' group, and even a full-blown healing center. I had begun writing ideas down on paper and shared them with my friend Diane, who had come to visit. I described for her my vision: a facility that offered a variety of resources to help people suffering from grief and loss. I envisioned a mental health library with big cozy furniture, a yoga/movement room, an art studio, a massage room, a counseling room, and a support group room. It was as if I had been dreaming of the details for years. This vision was so vivid in my mind that I felt I would burst if it didn't materialize. I felt like this dream was my lifeline, my way of finding new purpose in life.

As I continued with my counseling sessions and the fog of grief gradually began to lift, I started sharing thoughts of my vision with my counselor. She was immensely supportive of my ideas, especially because I was describing something that was direly needed in our society. I began speaking about my ideas with other the young widows I met on my path. One young widow in particular, Casey, became an amazing catalyst in helping me start my first support group.

About seven months after Brian's death, she rode with Ella and me to a ceremony in Washington, D.C., to honor Special Forces Medics who had died in combat. During the four-hour drive, I spoke in depth about my desire to create a strong connection with others "like us." Casey was in a life-coaching program at the time, and she encouraged me to go for it! She was my champion. I remember feeling chills on my skin and this intense motivation sweep over me as I came to the realization that I was answering my calling. I hadn't felt so excited since my daughter had been born. I thought, "I must be on the right path! These feelings are confirming it."

As soon as I returned from our trip, I began putting together a website that would help me reach the other young widows I was certain must be out there—not just in North Carolina but in the whole country, and I hoped, eventually, across the world. I had even picked out a name already. When I had first connected with my friend Tiffany online and found that our stories were so similar, she had referred to us as "soul widows." This name had stuck in my head as a powerful indicator of our connection, and this was also the message I wanted to give other widows who would come to my support group. I've never been very technologically oriented, but I was so determined to create an online community through which young widows could connect that I stayed up for hours every night for a week as I tirelessly worked on creating every single web page. I was so eager to get it out of my head and into the world! To this day, I am still not sure how I did it.

Once the website, www.SoulWidows.org, went live, I was finally able to exhale. Within just a few weeks, I began getting online visitors from across the country. A couple of women even sent me very personal emails about their own stories of loss. I was incredibly moved; their candidness touched my heart so deeply. I knew that if I helped only these few women, I would feel a sense of both peace and accomplishment.

As the group began to steadily grow, I began holding weekend retreats with a wonderful therapist, Mandy Eppley, who led the group sessions. Mandy is my business partner and also one of the coauthors of the heart-centered grief model I mentioned earlier in this chapter. I was fortunate to connect with her through my sister Jennifer, who had heard her speak as "Counselor Mandy" on a local Charlotte radio station. Jennifer felt that Mandy and I would have a lot in common and suggested that I meet with her. Upon meeting and sharing our stories, we realized that we shared a very similar vision of helping others through grief and helping them find hope again. I strongly believed in Mandy's therapeutic approach, so I asked her to become our official Soul Widows therapist. She enthusiastically accepted my request and has since been a very powerful and inspirational retreat leader for our Soul Widows retreat weekends.

I also involved my artist friend Diane, who came to lead the widows through healing art projects. Many of the women began attending the retreats on a regular basis. They are held at a gorgeous artist's haven in the small mountain town of Tryon, North Carolina. The inn is decorated with eclectic art from all over the world, and every room in the house has its own theme, among them an Egyptian theme, an equestrian theme, an angel theme, and a garden theme. The gourmet chef makes us home-cooked meals, and the owner of the inn brings us afternoon tea and cookies during our group sessions as well. My goal was for women to leave after the two days feeling nurtured and rejuvenated, and this goal is reached every time!

After getting the first taste of success with our inaugural Soul Widows retreat in July 2010, I knew without a doubt that I wanted to pursue my even larger goal. I wanted to create the center that I had envisioned in the early stages of my grief. Fortunately for me, Mandy held the same vision. She and I began talking in detail about what we wanted each room to look like and what group we wanted to serve. We felt that divine timing had brought us together to fulfill this mission, so with pure faith and determination, we began the process of seeking out an affordable space as our starting point. After a few weeks of looking in mid-July 2011, we settled on a beautiful little stone cottage (which I also call our Hobbit house). It had just the right number of rooms, and although it was rather small, we knew it would meet our needs for the time being.

Since we were going for this dream head-on, we began the process of applying for our nonprofit 501(c)3 status. Through the rigorous and painstakingly slow paperwork, Mandy introduced me to a long-time friend of hers, Cindy Ballaro, who could help us with the application. Cindy had worked with nonprofits for twenty-five years and had a very practical and grounded approach to business as a result. Cindy's skill sets and strengths perfectly complemented Mandy's and mine, and she agreed to join our team. This center has become our baby. I could not have done it without the combined effort of my amazing business partners.

In August 2011, we opened the doors of our labor of love, The Respite: A Centre for Grief & Hope (www.TheRespite.org). (In case you're curious, Mandy thought the British spelling of center had more elegance, and Cindy and I agreed.) It was surreal how quickly we had manifested our vision, and soon thereafter, other practitioners in the area wanted to be part of our organization by being added to our provider list. Everyone who walks through the doors of The Respite has told us the same thing: they feel instantly welcomed and nurtured by the space around them. Our goal was to be completely opposite from the clinical environment that pervades a lot of mental health clinics. Every room in our center is painted with vibrant colors and features cozy furniture and candles; from each ceiling hangs a lovely chandelier, and the walls are covered with original paintings and baroque art.

The mission statement for The Respite reads:

In an atmosphere of dignity and respect for the grief process, The Respite helps people, regardless of socioeconomic status, who have suffered a significant loss in any form to reclaim a healthy and productive life. We provide a safe haven, a supportive community, and take a holistic approach that offers a variety of healing modalities (mind, soul and body) to empower individuals and families. Our vision is to shift how grief is viewed in the world—moving from shame and isolation to unveiling (or mining) grief's transformative gifts. We welcome grief and provide hope for tomorrow.

In many ways, The Respite is like a one-stop shop for the bereaved. We offer traditional counseling, support groups, grief massage, restorative yoga, art therapy through SoulCollage®, aging/life transitions workshops, nutrition, personal training/body strengthening, workshops, retreats, and community gatherings. Soul Widows holds its meetings in our group room. Due to our desire to reach suffering people globally, we also launched webinars that allow people to log in from all over the world as we discuss different topics surrounding grief and loss. It is quite incredible to me that this center of compassion and understanding was born out of the two worst tragedies in my life. Talk about life's paradoxes!

Dear Friend,

I'm not suggesting that you have to go out and start a new organization in order to move forward in your healing process (unless you feel called in that direction, of course). I AM suggesting, however, that you listen to the creative spirit inside of you. Grief often calls us to create something out of our experience, no matter how small or big. You may find that when another friend or relative has a loss in their life, you happen to know just how to support them! You may have the words of solace to give to another person during their time of loss. It might amaze you how this makes your heart feel.

By going through a deep personal loss, and by following the path to healing, you are in fact equipped to a degree to lend support to others in the world. Do not forget how many other people across the earth are suffering! You are feeling something that is universal, and there are SO many people who don't know what to do with all their grief. It may not become clear to you right away what you are being called to do with your grief; you may simply become a wiser individual who can pass new life lessons on to your children. Your loss might impact the way you approach relationships as well as the pace at which you decide to pursue certain dreams.

Please do not let your grief hold you back from doing what your spirit is asking you to create! You have to first travel your grief journey before you can give back to the world. This is essential. But you may be surprised at how giving back to others through your own pain can bring an immense amount of healing to your own heart. Even if you have already been a volunteer or natural helper throughout your life, you will feel an even greater sense of healing and compassion after experiencing your loss. You may feel compelled to bring your gifts to a new level.

Consider this as food for thought if you find yourself asking at some point, "What now? What am I supposed to do with this journey, and what I have learned?" Everything comes with time so don't pressure yourself to go after things you don't feel ready for. Just remember, there is always something out there waiting that could use your energy and wisdom and special talents. We are all universally connected, so when and if you feel called to share your gifts, there is no doubt you will impact the universe tenfold!

Love and Light,
Elizabeth B.

"Creativity can lead to incredible healing.
Stay open to new ways of addressing
your grief—whether spiritually,
mentally, or physically."
—Elizabeth B.

"Eventually and consciously, we adjust
to the loss and emerge with new direction.
We accept and mature emotionally. We forge
new relationships and beginnings. We spend
more time on the living than on the loss, more
time in the present than in the past, and we are
rewarded with growth that ushers us forward
with renewed intensity and purpose."
—Carol P.

What doesn't kill you makes you stronger (whether you like it or not)

> It always seems impossible until it's done.
> —NELSON MANDELA

IN THE BEGINNING OF my journey, I felt very weak in every sense of the word—physically, mentally, and emotionally. However, as I managed step-by-step to overcome obstacles that came across my path (with the help of family, friends, counseling, and support groups), I grew stronger. A phenomenal network of caring people has held me up and encouraged me, and my own individual sense of self-belief has pushed me forward. There are times when I've doubted my abilities to be able to "make it." But I've realized through my transformative grief process that a fulfilling life after loss is possible.

When it comes right down to it, I realize that life has too many amazing things to offer, and I'm not willing to miss out on those gifts and adventures because I've had tragedies in my life. Yes, I still occasionally get my daughter to preschool two hours late because I'm simply too physically and emotionally exhausted to get ready on time. Yes, I still have an uncanny ability to forget details, such as what day it is or certain memories. And yes, I do have periods during certain seasons when I tend to get more emotional and retreat from the world for a while. I usually feel a wave of grief that begins right after Christmas as I anticipate the anniversary of my son's death in late January, and then again in August. But I know that these are a natural part of my healing process and coping with the post-traumatic stress that happens after a loss. I'm able to name all the areas in which I greatly lack perfection, but I've given myself the gift of being able to either laugh at them or simply remind myself of my humanity. And despite those lapses, I love and accept myself for where I am right now.

Even though I've gained a sense of strength through unfortunate circumstances, I feel like I've been armored to take life head-on. It's as if I've been initiated into a club that no one wants to belong to but one that has given me a badge of honor. It is all too easy for bereaved people to retreat into alcohol and drugs or to avoid social contact and disconnect themselves from life. I want to embrace those who have taken that path and rescue them, even though I know it's up to them to make that decision.

I knew that I had two choices: I could withdraw into my pain and escape from reality (which I knew would hit me at some point even if I tried to run from it), or I could walk into the storm, take the punches and bruises, open my heart to acceptance and healing, and continue on a new adventure. Throughout my journey, I've reached various milestones that have marked my growing strength—moving into my first apartment, seeking counseling, attending support groups, creating new relationships and deepening old ones, beginning Soul Widows, cofounding The Respite, opening my heart to love again, and sharing my story with numerous strangers in the hope that it will lend strength, belief, and hope to others. Recording my milestones as I've walked through my grief journey has helped me, plain and simple. Whenever I've felt tempted to fall into a dark mental space, I often go through the list of what I've already done to remind myself of what's possible. At times, I need to "check in" with myself to stay on track.

I can't tell you how often I've said to myself, "I'm so tired of having to be strong! Why can't someone else be strong for me instead?"

I know it's important to have strong insightful people around me, but no one is in charge of running my life except for me. There are so many different elements in my life that need to be balanced, such as being a mother, handling responsibilities at The Respite, managing Soul Widows, and evolving from the lessons of my grief journey. So, I need to check in with myself once in a while to make sure I'm not pushing myself unnecessarily. It can be easy to get caught up in the whirlwind of life and forget to take a breather, to truly be present in my experiences. I must use methods to protect my energy so that I don't burn out! Sometimes this involves quiet meditation, reading an inspirational book, taking a walk, doing yoga, dancing, enjoying time with family, or saying prayers and connecting with the "Divine," the greater energy that I believe connects us all.

I use my creativity to find balance amid my grief and joy. After all, I cannot have one without the other. Even though there were times when I might have wished to hand my pain over to someone else to hold for a while, I would not want to have missed out on the gifts that were revealed by staying on my own path of growth. Sharing my experiences now might give another woman the strength to make it through her day, and she in turn might help another. This has helped motivate me, even through moments of great pain, to live an open-hearted existence. I believe I gather strength from the generations of women who came before me—that together we all hold the suffering of the world. This image helps me feel "held" in my story, knowing that others have thrived despite adversity. It has empowered me to strive to be an example of creative, fearless, and wholehearted living. This is certainly a challenge! Yet it's a positive challenge that I work toward each day, as I step further into the unknown with curiosity and wonder. By continuing to walk into the unknown, I've learned to become proud of my strength, because I wouldn't have gotten this far without it!

Dear Friend,

You're strength should be celebrated. It does not always feel good to hear the admiring "you're so strong" sentences from those who haven't experienced loss, but I do feel that your resilience should be acknowledged in a positive way. This may come in the form of being reminded by those closest to you what you have gone through, and what you have accomplished since your loss. If you are very early in your loss, simply getting out of bed in the morning, getting the kids to school, or cooking a meal should be treated as GREAT accomplishments. If you have moved farther on your grief journey, having continued with close relationships, perhaps making new friends, and staying at a job or taking a new one should be treated as GREAT accomplishments. If you have been through months or years of your healing process and have helped others through the wisdom you have gained, gone on new adventures, taken new risks, and found joy on the way, that is beautiful and amazing!

I believe it's important to check in with yourself to consistently see how you're doing. Even on days when you feel like you have completely fallen apart, if you continue to get back up and keep trying you are tapping into your inner strength. Don't be surprised by the people who may look up to you. You might find yourself in the position of being someone's mentor, or talking her through a situation that you yourself once thought overwhelming. Your wisdom is your strength. Your tears are your strength. Your ability to move forward despite the odds is your strength. And your strength is beautiful, and I deeply honor it!

Love and Light,

Elizabeth B.

"We are not given 'things'; we are given strength."

—Edith H.

"You never know how strong you are . . . until being strong is the only choice you have."

—Tracy P.

Did I really just say that?

Become the sky. Take an axe to the prison wall. Escape. Walk out like someone suddenly born into color. Do it now.

—RUMI

I HAVE BEEN AMAZED by some of the things that have come out of my mouth since the beginning of my journey through grief. I'm not talking about all the negative, angry things that often came out in the very beginning, but the words of gratitude and gratefulness that have flowed out so many times. While I can never be grateful for the loss of a loved one, I can say that I am deeply grateful for the life experiences, deep love, and wisdom that my grief has brought me.

I used to think that I would never say the words "I am happy" ever again. Yet, every day when I look at Ella delighting in something, I am filled with an indescribable happiness. Sometimes I think my chest will burst with the fullness of love that I feel. It's strong enough to melt any sadness or anger away. I think, "Right now, in this very moment, this is good."

I can also say, "I'm grateful for the lessons that this grief has brought me." I have come to appreciate my humanness, capabilities, resiliency, creativity, and desire to experience the world in a very deep way. I often find myself thinking or saying, "I can't believe the blessings that have come to me through these two tragedies." I never would have met the amazing and inspirational people who have come across my path. I wouldn't be doing the important work that I'm doing or be living to my full potential. I never reached for life with the same determination that I have now.

I feel that I've also found my voice. I've seen so many different sides of life, and experienced so many different feelings and parts of myself, that I now know myself in a very intimate way. At times I felt like things were moving so fast—nothing short of super speed!—I was falling off the tracks, but I've finally harnessed the power behind what I've been learning. I still have countless miles to go, but I've found that the more I embrace life and work on trusting myself and others, the more the blessings unfold in miraculous ways.

Many times when it seemed my life had crumbled into pieces around me, there was always a new chapter opening up for me. Somehow, the puzzle has always worked itself out. I've begun to view life as an adventure. There are always going to be ups and down, trials and ecstasy. Even after going through such devastating and heart-wrenching losses, I would still rather feel things and live life to the fullest rather than hide in a cave and attempt to protect myself from the uncertainties of the world. I don't feel that would be a wise role model for those I care about, either. The truth is, we never know what life will bring us and we don't have as much control as we might think we have. But we CAN choose how we walk through life and how we spend our time.

As I continue to walk my transformative journey, I've finally been able to say that I'm excited about what comes next. I actually look forward to what is around the corner. I used to feel afraid of the future, always assuming the worst. But now I've realized that my worst fears have already happened, and I've survived them! I've walked into the fire and made it out alive. Only the loss of a close loved one could have "woken me up" to reality in the same way.

On many occasions, I've said to myself there is nothing like feeling truly "awake" and aware of my life and what it means to me. I also look forward to living in honor of my loved ones and the love and belief that they brought to me. So I look ahead and think, "There is still so much to be done, and I will continue to make the most of it."

Dear Friend,

You might eventually find yourself thinking and saying things that you once never thought possible. As you continue to move through your grief and evolve in your healing, you might be overcome by moments of gratitude. These might come in the form of someone reaching out to you, a beautiful sunny day, or your decision to initiate a new project or adventure. These feelings of gratefulness can come from anywhere. You may not be aware of them at first, but it is important to allow them in and acknowledge them—even if only for a fleeting moment. As soon as you have a positive thought, write it down. On days when you're feeling sad or feel as if you are moving backward—and we all have those days—it may help to think about what you feel grateful for, such as certain supportive people in your life or new resources you have found to assist you in your grief process.

I continue to be amazed by the words I hear around me as I'm leading my support groups. Some women who have recently lost their spouse come in saying how lucky they were to have had such an incredible partner in their life. Some women have told me that they've become more in touch with themselves and have pursued traveling or trying new things they never before felt capable of. I've also met several women who have told me, "I truly feel happy again," or "I never thought I could find as deep a love and connection with someone else, but I've come to realize that it does exist!" It's exciting to see such beautiful, strong, broken-open, life-loving women who have been through the depths of sorrow and have risen through the experience to embrace more amazing things in front of them.

My hope for you is that you will remain open to these possibilities and TRUST that life will bring more blessings to you. So many women have walked in our shoes before us, and they have proven time and again that joy IS possible after loss. I hold strong to this belief and work on walking in it every day. I invite you to walk with me! Remember, you never have to go forward alone!

Love and Light,
Elizabeth B.

"Remember how beautiful and amazing you are and that you bring unique gifts to the world. You may serve as a role model for others in the future through all that you embrace on your journey."

—Elizabeth B.

"Grief is the great gateway into our deepest truth of who we are, what we're made of, where we are being led. It will catapult us onto a life of greater and deeper meaning if we let go and stop fighting the feelings of grief. Trust your grief; it is a great messenger sent to teach you about the inner deep mysteries of your own brilliant and beautiful spirit."

—Mandy E.

Afterword

Elizabeth's story touches us very profoundly. Her great loss, her shattering pain, her journey through grief, and her ongoing resurrection of spirit evoke in us empathy, a deep sense of solidarity, and great hope. I have the privilege of knowing Elizabeth personally. I am very impressed and inspired by how she sculpted her story as a vessel for life—life with its tragedies and with its joy and creative vitality. Elizabeth has been intimate with tears. She also never lost her radiant smile and her will to birth a blessing out of the womb of her suffering, a blessing for herself, for her family, and for the world. A vision was born for her: the Soul Widows group and the cocreation of The Respite: A Centre for Grief & Hope. Hers is a testimony about the journey of the heart through grief. If we hold our grief as sacred, we are sculpted by it. We become more loving and caring human beings. We are guided to our noblest vision of service. We find our solidarity with others who suffer.

Unfortunately, the values of our modern culture do not encourage us to respect our grief nor to hold our grief as sacred. Most of the messages we receive are to "get over it" as quickly as we can, to keep "a stiff upper lip," to numb our sorrow through overdrinking, drugs, or medicine. Our sadness, anguish, and anger in our grief, are perceived as negative if not part of a malady to be cured. Negative? A malady? When our ability to feel is one of the most significant features of our evolution! When the greatest achievements of our civilization came from people who were able to feel deeply their own grief and the grief of others! Where would we be if Martin Luther King Jr. and his partners in the Civil Rights movement had not allowed themselves to feel their grief and its anguish? How would we have great art, amazing music, and astounding humanitarian work if people's hearts were not broken open by grief and, more important, if they did not permit themselves to be transformed by the depth of that grief? The cost of denying our grief is just too high. It is untenable on a personal, a spiritual, and a social level.

Grief is a painful experience and yet a holy experience that humanizes us and matures our vision of service. Ultimately, the story of our grief is the story of the heart, of love and the emerging passion to serve the world. We all stand in gratitude to Elizabeth and people like her who did the work to let rivers of love flow through their heart wounds.

Mandy Eppley and I wrote *The Model of Heart-Centered Grief* to support people in their journey of grief and hope. We both have worked for decades with individuals whose hearts were broken by some misfortune or other. We realized how depleted people were from the underlying shame they had about their own grief. Bombarded with messages that asserted that happiness is the only worthwhile feeling, they felt that their time of sorrow cheated them out of a full life. In addition to all that we learned as psychotherapists and spiritual coaches, Mandy and I experienced a great deal of wounding in our own lives both as children and as adults. We knew also the pain resulting from devaluing our own grief.

Thankfully we later experienced the power of walking the grief journey with an open heart, mining the numerous gifts of that grief and heeding the call to serve, a call emerging out of the wounds inflicted on our spirit. That is why our heart-centered grief model stresses: "Know that your grief is sacred. Let your heart be opened to the initiation that your grief is guiding you through." We wanted to emphasize the psychological dynamics of grief and hope and also the rich spiritual meaning and astounding spiritual gifts of such a journey.

I offer you this meditation in respect and support for your own challenges and grief:

> Your wounds hold the seeds of your greatest blessings. You are reborn in the turmoil of your greatest sorrows. Trust in the ability of the Divine to transform everything for your growth and enrichment of spirit. Nothing will be allowed to hurt you without the tears of your pain becoming, with time, jewels of the heart. We are learning to become peaceful in the midst of storms. For we know that the hand of the loving God never lets go of ours, even when our darkest hours overwhelm us with doubt and despair. Your spirit will always be revived and anointed with love. That is the ineffable promise. That is the unshakeable bond between your heart and the heart of the Divine.

With gratitude to Elizabeth, The Respite, and all those who have birthed from their wounds a greater love and a wider solidarity with those who suffer and struggle,

CHRIS SAÂDE
Author of *Second Wave Spirituality: Passion for Peace, Passion for Justice*
Codirector of the Olive Branch Center

Creative Hip Chick Ideas: Activities to Nurture Your Spirit

> If you're alive you're creative . . . we "reduce" and "deflect" our creative selves in many ways. Life is the creative act, not the canvas or the blank page.
>
> —PATTI DIGH

Dear Friend,

This list of "Creative Hip Chick Ideas" was developed from some of the activities I created and practiced throughout different stages of my own grief journey. Several of the suggestions have also come from women who participate in Soul Widows or from our clients at The Respite. You might be thinking, "But I don't have a creative bone in my body!" Well, the beauty of these activities is that you don't have to be an artist or expert at anything. As author Patti Digh has said, "If you're alive, you're creative." Plus, all these activities are optional. You may find that some of the creative ideas resonate with you and others don't. Feel free to do one activity or all of them! It's completely up to you. You may find you are drawn to do certain activities early in your grief and then gradually feel up to pursuing other ideas later on in your journey as your needs shift and your grief is transformed. Although you may initially engage in an activity as a distraction, you may find that you feel uplifted by it and strengthened to try other ones.

I have divided the "Creative Hip Chick Ideas" into three categories:

- **Being Mindful** includes writing, music, list-making, and self-nurturing activities. They are about being gentle with yourself and being mindful of your thoughts and needs while pulling from your creative spirit.

- **Getting Physical** recommends activities that can help improve your overall well-being through movement. Because grief is often held in the body, these activities can help release stress and muscle tension while also providing relaxation for the mind. They can be done at any level of fitness, and they are also a great reason to get up and get going during the day!

- **Going Visual** lists fun art activities that can be done by anyone. They include projects such as making a memory scrapbook, wishing ribbons, or decorating affirmation stones. Remember, you don't need to consider yourself an "artist" to be creative!

Be as free with all of these activities as you like. Do them at your own pace; do them by yourself or with a friend; do them early in the morning or in the middle of the night; do one a day or one every three months. Let your spirit loose and make these activities *yours*. You might be amazed by what you create or are able to do. There is a creative hip chick in all of us, I promise!

With big love on your creative
and transformative journey,
Elizabeth B.

Being Mindful

Keep a journal.

Some women find it easier to express their thoughts and feelings through words rather than through music or a fine art. And it doesn't matter whether you start writing the day your loved one dies or the day of the funeral or several months into your journey of grief. Use journaling as a tool when you need it. Make it a friend who listens to you in the absence of your partner who used to be your sounding board. And listen to it as it beckons you to get out of bed, splash water in your face, and commit some of your heavy sadness or anger or perplexity to paper—on pages no one but you will ever read. As with scrapbooking, you can choose to make your journal as simple or as elaborate as you want to. Suggest to those who want to help you through your grieving but are at a loss as to what to do that they give you a pretty journal as a gift.

Create a CD that speaks to your soul.

Like me, you might be caught off guard if you're driving somewhere with the radio on and a song or instrumental music that makes you sad comes on. Having a CD or two that you've recorded with music that calms or distracts you, either one, puts that in your control. Further along in your grieving process you might even draw a lot of comfort from a CD of your loved one's favorite songs, or ones that you enjoyed together or that bring back special memories. Never underestimate the healing power of music.

Seek a little comfort just for you.

As you've read in numerous places in this book, it's extremely important for you to find little things that bring you a measure of comfort and joy in the midst of your sorrow. If you haven't found a particular comfort yet, I urge you to start looking for one. Try a new coffee flavor, treat yourself to a little extravagance—whether it's Godiva chocolate or an ounce of exotic perfume—or splurge on a mani-pedi. Check out a new TV or book series that one of your friends recommended. Find something that might take you out of your head and away from your heavy heart, even for just a bit. The only criterion is that it should make you smile. You know best what you're ready for and how to give yourself such a gift of kindness now and again.

Eat!

That's right, I said "Eat!" One of the first things we do when we're in the depths of emotional pain or numbness is to forget to eat. Or we know we need to eat to keep up our strength, but food is tasteless and has absolutely no appeal. To help stir up an appetite, literally, I suggest you grab a bite of food from one of your favorite restaurants. If it's a place you ate at routinely with your loved one, which will awaken too many sad thoughts and feelings, then find a new restaurant or trendy eatery where you've never eaten before. Invite a relative or friend along for the adventure. If you don't feel like leaving the house, though, have a friend or family member grab a takeout meal for the two of you and share it together at your kitchen table. (Don't eat in bed if you can help it.) Try to make the meal as healthy as possible—but you're entitled to a little dessert too!

**Write down all the ways you were
enriched by your loved one in your life.**

What did your loved one teach you? You may be enriched by the way
your loved one championed your spirit while he or she was alive:
perhaps by influencing your career path or sparking a new life passion; by loving you unconditionally as a daughter, mother, sister, or
wife; or by teaching you a new way of viewing the world or yourself.
By writing down all the ways you were enriched, you may begin to
appreciate elements of your life more, even amid the sadness. It is also
another way to honor your loved one's life and death by emulating
the enriching aspects that he or she brought to you. You may even be
inspired to enrich others in your life in similar ways.

Learn to make lists.

And one of the first should be a list of the things you feel you "need"
right now in order to prevent you from becoming overwhelmed
in your grief. These needs may include money, housing, childcare,
counseling, and so on. Take a sheet of notebook paper or use a clean
page in your journal and list your needs either in random order or
from highest to lowest priority. Leave a blank line or two in between
the items. Then go back through the list and answer this question:
Is this need being met? If yes, add how or by whom. Then ask and
answer a second, related question: Will this change in the near future?
If not, write down steps you need to take to become more courageously direct in asking others to help you get the support you need.
You may find that your list of needs changes over time, so it may help
to revisit the list now and again to add new needs or ways that a current need being met should be changed.

Another type of list could be called "Personal Self-Care." It could
include such items as choosing an exercise, getting your hair done,
taking a bubble bath, eating healthy foods, etc. Then make a point
to make time for these ideas and put a checkmark by them. At The

Respite we have a wonderful class for those grieving a recent loss called "Self-Care during the First Year." It offers all sorts of great self-nurturing tips. (Visit www.TheRespite.org for more details.) This is so important for your overall well-being and resiliency.

Spend time around animals.
Why? Because recent studies show that interacting with animals can increase our levels of oxytocin, the hormone that helps human beings "feel happy and trusting." It also "has some powerful effects [upon] the body's ability to be in a state of readiness to heal, and also to grow new cells, so it predisposes us to an environment in our own bodies where we can be healthier."* And when we are physically stronger, we can become emotionally healthier too, I think. A visit to a farm, a zoo, or a nature center where you have the opportunity to see animals that you don't see every day can be very therapeutic. Try to go during a time of day or during a season when it's not too busy. For those of you who like horses, go horseback riding! Don't forget to consider getting a pet if circumstances allow. Once again, studies reveal that caring for a pet, such as a cat or a dog, can "ease loneliness, reduce stress, promote social interaction, encourage exercise and playfulness, and provide us with unconditional love and affection"—all of which help us deal with grieving. (If you choose a pet from the SPCA or another type of animal rescue shelter, you'll have the double benefit of helping a good cause as you help yourself.)

Treat yourself to something you've been wanting.
A very good sign that you are emerging from your shock and deep distress is when you start to think about something, anything, else! Don't restrict how great or how small the special something has to be. It could be phoning a landscape architect to discuss designing a

---

* Julie Rovner, Pet Therapy: How Animals Heal Each Other, NPR.org (http://www.m.npr.org/story/146583986), accessed May 29, 2013.

memorial garden in your yard. It could be buying a special piece of jewelry you and your loved one talked about buying for your next anniversary. It could be ordering a new dress you recall seeing in a catalog just before your partner died. Or it could simply be indulging in a cup of exotic coffee at your favorite café. Sometimes something new can feel refreshing. For instance, many months into my grief process one thing I loved to do when I would travel was to purchase a piece of jewelry that was symbolic of my grief, such as a ring with a black gemstone. You might consider getting a necklace or ornament with your loved one's initials or a meaningful symbol engraved on it as a keepsake item.

Create a ritual of honor during a holiday, birthday, anniversary, or other celebration.

For example, light a candle for your loved one on each of these special days. Or decorate something in remembrance of the one who died. Every Christmas, my sister Megan decorates a mini tree in honor of my son. She saw an owl on the morning that Tookie died, so she believes that owls represent his spirit. She hangs different owl ornaments on her mini tree each year, and this has become her beautiful ritual to pay tribute to her nephew. Other ideas for a remembrance ritual on special occasions include: watching his or her favorite movie; donating to a charity of his or her choosing; hosting a special lunch or dinner in your beloved's honor; planting a tree or perennial flowering shrub; and inviting friends and neighbors to an informal ceremony at your loved one's gravesite or memorial site.

Learn a new game with your girlfriends.

One of my personal favorites is the Go Goddess! game. This board game features cards that ask you reflective questions about different areas of your life. It is best to play it with a group of women you have already established trust with so that it is easier to be candid and authentic. The insightful questions may help you reflect on things that need more attention and can lead to interesting discussion and even moments of support, validation, and empowerment from connecting with your close women friends. There are also many opportunities for laughter! I also suggest playing this game while you serve refreshments and delicious food (like fondue!).

Practice random acts of kindness.

Read any list of what makes people happy and you'll find a variation on the notion that we derive happiness from supporting other people. As author Leo Bormans put it, "just as other people can make us happy, we are all 'other people' to someone else." When you are growing a little bored and restless with staying in bed all day or not venturing out of your house, think about reaching out to others to help lift you from your own grief. One way to do so is through a charitable act. Look through your cabinets and closets for any extra kitchen items or articles of clothing you don't need anymore. This may even include clothing from your deceased spouse's/partner's wardrobe. By donating clothing to others in need, you will both honor that loved one and feel good about helping a fellow man or woman who is coping with all that life can throw at them. One avenue that helped lift me up from the depths of my grief was to create Soul Widows. This allowed me to directly connect with other women in pain and to look outside of my own grief and sadness. Being aware that others were out there going through similar experiences reminded me that I was not alone, and it showed me the power of community. It buoyed my spirits to know that I was making an effort for the greater good of others. Suddenly, my path wasn't as lonely.

Consider writing your own story of loss and hope!

This may sound like an overwhelming statement to some, but there are so many creative ways to access the "writer" inside you. You don't have to be a master at language or have a degree in literature to do this. Anyone can be an author of her own story, whether through journaling, talking about your memories into a recorder, writing poems, displaying your words on art canvases or stationery, or simply jotting thoughts down on sticky notes! There is no right or wrong way to do it. I started by simply writing down memories of my experiences. As I wrote down the specific memories, the details surrounding events gradually came back to me. My thoughts and ideas also evolved out of conversations with girlfriends or women I've met in support groups. You might be interested in taking a life story writing workshop, as one of the women in my Soul Widows group did, seeking a writing coach, or interviewing influential people in your life. You might become inspired by simply reading about the journeys of others. You might like to write your story just for yourself or for the purpose of sharing it. If you did so, who would your audience be? There are endless ways to tell your story. If you become stuck with one method, then try another. If there comes a moment when you feel inspired, go to town! You never know what may evolve and what treasures you might find along the way.

Getting Physical

Visit a massage therapist.

Massage is a phenomenal healing tool. We often don't even recognize how much emotional tension we store in our muscles as we are working through the grief process. At The Respite, we offer what is called Grief Massage, which is an approach that focuses on deep relaxation, presence, and intention for clients who have experienced loss or are recovering from another type of emotional trauma. Our Grief Massage program is quite unique, and you can learn more about it at www.TheRespite.org.

If you are unable to visit our center, however, it is possible to find a licensed massage therapist near you who can tailor a partial or full-body massage to your needs. I asked The Respite's massage therapist, Aimee Joy Taylor, for her suggestions, and this is what she shared:

> Finding a compassionate and skilled massage therapist for the grief journey can often be done through referrals or word of mouth. Ask friends, colleagues, even your clergy or grief counselor for recommendations. Let them know what you are looking for: a licensed massage therapist who specializes in deep relaxation and is comfortable working with the grief process. If word of mouth doesn't work, call your local hospital and find out if they offer a massage program. You may also consider seeking out a massage therapist who volunteers with your local hospice organization or provides Oncology Massage at one

of your local hospitals. Working with clients who are facing serious illness or end-of-life care can help a massage therapist develop the presence and intention that is needed for Grief Massage. Or, go online and search one of the following massage therapist referral networks: The American Massage Therapy Association (www.amtamassage.org) or Associated Bodywork and Massage Professionals (www.abmp.com). A massage therapist with several years of relaxation massage is recommended. You may work with several before finding a match that feels right. That is a normal and healthy way to find what works best for you.

Go treat yourself. You deserve it!

Travel.
If you are able to get away from your usual surroundings for a while, it can be a welcome breath of fresh air. Perhaps your first trip after you lose a loved one should be in the company of a cherished family member or friend. This can be a simple weekend getaway or a more extensive vacation. You'll recall that I traveled with a few women friends to Jamaica about seven months after my husband's death. It was incredibly soothing to listen to the waves and to feel the warmth of the sun. I suggest bringing a girlfriend and some sunscreen! Another type of travel is to visit your loved one's family members or friends that you enjoyed together as couples. Yet another excuse to travel is to attend a special retreat for the purpose of creative grieving (see the list at the end of the book for such resources) or to indulge at a health spa where you are pampered and waited on from sunup to sundown. Two wonderful retreats tailored to grief, loss, and healing are the Soul Widows Retreat (www.SoulWidows.org) and Golden Willow Retreat: A Sanctuary for Grief & Loss (www.goldenwillow-retreat.org). For more of a spa experience, you may want to look into

Holistic Spa Retreats at www.our-healing-hub.com or visit www.healinglifestyles.com.

Become a day-tripper.

On your own or with a friend or relative, visit a place within fifty miles of your home that you've never been before. Enjoy the whole process of investigating what's close to home—museums, historical sites, parks, recreational opportunities, and shops and eateries—and then planning your day away accordingly. This is a great way to get to know someone from your support group or to draw comfort from a longtime friend. But, whether you go alone or with a companion, this will stretch you in a healthy way, and it can reassure you that life goes on and that you want to join in on it.

Try a creative movement/dance class.

You don't have to be a dancer to receive the therapeutic benefits of moving your body to music! There is a very powerful form of therapeutic dance called the 5 Rhythms, which was created by Gabrielle Roth, who distinguished five rhythms she believed are common to all humans: flowing, staccato, chaos, lyrical, and stillness. She discovered that these rhythms liberate the creative spirit inside of us, regardless of our physical ability, size, or age. The 5 Rhythms are described as "a practice, both poetic and practical, fluid and focused, a marriage of art and healing that directly addresses the divorce of body from heart, heart from mind that has so plagued our cultures." This type of dancing is often described as a "moving meditation." Another great aspect to this type of dance is that there is no choreography or steps to learn, and no way of doing it wrong! This practice has become worldwide. To find a workshop or class near you, visit www.gabrielleroth.com.

You can also seek out a dance therapist if you wish to find a dance therapy group that focuses on a specific issue, such as loss, or to do a one-on-one session. The American Dance Therapy Association defines dance/movement therapy as "the psychotherapeutic use of movement to promote emotional, social, cognitive, and physical integration of the individual. Dance therapists focus on helping their clients improve self-esteem and body image, develop effective communication skills and relationships, expand their movement vocabulary, gain insight into patterns of behavior, as well as create new options for coping with problems." To find a dance therapist or group near you visit www.adta.org.

Take a yoga class!

At The Respite, we offer a class called Restorative Yoga. Grieving can cause all sorts of aches and pains in our bodies. Through practicing yoga, there is an opportunity to release the tension and stress that can build up as grief experiences are processed. We describe Restorative Yoga as "a place to release, revitalize, and relax as we focus on meditative breathing practices, positive mantras, and healing postures. This type of yoga is gentle and suitable for beginners. Combined with mindfulness and meditation, this can help you find more balance within by calming the overactive mind." Our yoga practitioner, Cat Babbie, says, "Restorative and Yin Yoga are the best types of yoga for someone grieving. They are the most gentle on the body and allow for time to meditate and breathe. Learning to acknowledge and control your breath helps you react to stress (and grief) in a gentler, calmer way." If you are an experienced yogi, then keeping up with your practice can greatly benefit you on your grief journey. It is another powerful act of self-care! To learn more about Restorative Yoga at The Respite visit www.TheRespite.org. To find yoga classes, workshops, and retreats near you, go to www.yogafinder.com or www.yogatoday.com.

Going Visual

Create a memory scrapbook.

Believe me, you don't have to be an artist to make one of these. I suggest working on it while you are listening to soothing music and lighting some candles to create an inviting space. A good place to start is to gather letters, greeting cards, notes, postcards, photographs, and any other meaningful memorabilia from your life together. Then sort them chronologically or thematically, for example. In the scrapbook I created for my son, I used his baby album and glued in cards from his memorial and sweet drawings from my nieces and nephew in his honor, and then I filled out the sections that related to my pregnancy with him. In my late husband's scrapbook, I created a chronological story of his life through pictures and letters so that his daughters can look back and see his life story someday. Take some time to arrange and rearrange your collection to suit your sense of design and aesthetics, even if others won't see it. This will be your private and very personal way of honoring the memory of your loved one.

You needn't invest in expensive albums, by the way, but if the idea of a professional-looking album appeals to you, let your family and friends know they can buy you an attractive album as a gift. Because scrapbooking has become such a popular hobby, they should easily find a shop or an online outlet (scrapbook.com offers numerous varieties, for instance) through which they can purchase one. Give yourself time to reread the love letters and cards or to study the photographs as you make your scrapbook pages. And don't be afraid for the therapeutic tears to flow as you do so; they are such an important part of expressing your great sorrow. The beauty of a scrapbook is that you'll have a great collection of keepsakes that you can open whenever you want or need to take a walk down memory lane again.

Take a creative art class.

Many therapists and laypeople alike now know that the visual arts—whether painting, drawing, making masks or collages—are a powerful tool through which we can express and manage our feelings of grief. One great place to visit is the women's online community www.BraveGirlsClub.com. There you'll read descriptions of some wonderful online classes you can pursue in the comfort of your own home. They also offer fabulous artistic retreats for those who want a change of scenery while they participate with others in Brave Girls Club's in-person programs. Even if you've never considered yourself to be "artistic," you can learn. And you may discover that applying colors to any surface lets you unleash your grief pains in a cleansing and satisfying way.

Create an altar in honor of your loved one's life and death.

As Karla Helbert, MS, LPC, wrote in her article titled "Creating Shrines and Altars for Healing from Grief," those terms can be used interchangeably, but: "If religious connotations make you uncomfortable, you may wish to think of a personally created altar or shrine as a memorial, memory box, memory space, honoring space, remembering space, meditation space, etc. Your space can be called whatever you choose to call it." I recommend that you visit http://www.goodtherapy.org/blog/shrine-altar-grief-healing/to read Ms. Helbert's full article, in which she includes a list of ideas that may help you in the process of creating a special place in your home—or even a portable shrine you carry with you—where you can reflect on your loved one in a personal ritual as well as heal from the pain of your loss. Among the many items you might choose from for your altar are photos, special objects that hold significance in relation to your memories of that person, flowers, and candles. It is important to keep the memories alive, for there is great comfort through remembrance.

Create a memory box.
Just as in making a memory scrapbook, you can collect sacred mementos that remind you how special your loved one was and how lucky you were to know him or her. Place these items in a keepsake or memory box. You can repurpose a shoebox or cardboard box by decorating it with any mixed media—cloth, felt, original artwork, collage or decoupage—you wish. Or buy an inexpensive plastic bead box for items that won't fit into a two-dimensional album. Enjoy making it pretty and unique! Two great places to visit online for ideas or to buy fabrics and craft supplies are Joann.com or Michaels.com. Or make it known to your circle of caregivers that you'd love to receive a ready-made keepsake box or the materials with which to make your own.

Make a memorial quilt from your loved one's clothing.
As one online resource (www.recover-from-grief.com.) puts it, "wrap yourself in loving memories." I recommend that you visit this website for touching stories and ideas about the various ways parents, siblings, spouses, and friends can cope with the death of a loved one through this type of creative grieving. Consider either sewing a pillow covering or a full-size quilt by yourself or asking someone you trust, such as a friend, family member, or experienced quilter who honors your loss, to work with you on it.

Try your hand at SoulCollage®.
I can't say enough good things about it, and if you haven't heard of this wonderful therapeutic art, you have a pleasant surprise in store

for you. The best part is, you don't have to be an artist. It is a process of taking a 3x5 piece of cardstock (which you yourself can cut out from a box or poster board) onto which you paste images you cut out of old magazines to make a collage that inspires and speaks to you. I experienced SoulCollage® for the first time about four years into my grief journey and found that it deeply resonated with several different aspects of my life. I was able to directly address my emotions about losing my loved ones, and I found that the meaning within the cards was applicable to all areas of my life. The experience was very nurturing and affirming. For more information on SoulCollage® classes, visit www.TheRespite.org. To find workshops near you or for online classes, visit www.soulcollage.com.

Decorate stones with affirmations.

Gather smooth stones from outdoors and paint or draw affirmations on them such as "I am incredible," "Trust," or "Be still." You can display them in a bowl and leave them in a place where you will see them daily. As the examples I've given show, the affirmations should center on you and your striving to express your grief in a healthy way. Find proverbs or sayings that encourage you and lift your spirit too. Variations on stone painting include painting inspirational sayings on old boards or bookshelves; writing them on squares of fabric or flags using special pens; or taking a china painting class in which you substitute the affirmation for a decorative design.

Create wishing ribbons.

Gather some spools of wide, sturdy ribbons in your favorite colors. Using a Sharpie, write down your hopes or wishes and tie the ribbons to a tree (or trees) in your yard or from a porch railing. There are many meanings to be found through creating these ribbons: They can simply add a dose of beautiful color to brighten your environment. They might be viewed like Tibetan prayer flags, which are believed to send the energy of what is written on the flags into the wind and will bring happiness, joy, and good health to others. Or making ribbons could become a ritual with which to honor your loved one during special times of the year. You are free to create your own meaning!

Your Creative Grieving
TOOLBOX

GRIEF SUPPORT

The Respite: A Centre for Grief & Hope
  www.TheRespite.org

The Model of Heart-Centered Grief DVD Series
  www.TheRespite.org

Soaring Spirits Loss Foundation
  www.sslf.org

SupportWorks
  www.supportworks.org

Open to Hope
  www.opentohope.com

Heartache to Healing Grief Support
  www.heartachetohealing.com

Center for Loss & Life Transition
www.centerforloss.com

The Grief Project
www.griefproject.org

OUR HOUSE Grief Support Center
www.ourhouse-grief.org

Daily Strength
www.dailystrength.org

Grief's Journey
www.griefsjourney.com

Grief and Renewal
www.griefandrenewal.com

The Light Beyond
www.thelightbeyond.com

Web Healing
www.webhealing.com

The Dougy Center
www.dougy.org

CancerCare
www.cancercare.org

Golden Willow Retreat Center
www.goldenwillowretreat.org

LOSS OF A SPOUSE/PARTNER

Soul Widows
www.Soulwidows.org

American Widow Project

www.americanwidowproject.org

Widows Wear Stilettos

www.widowswearstilettos.org

Young Widow

www.youngwidow.org

The Widdahood

www.thewiddahood.com

Lesbian Widow Support

www.lesbianwidowsupport.com

The United Warrior Survivor Foundation

www.neverquitneverforget.org

Gold Star Wives of America, Inc.

www.goldstarwives.org

LOSS OF A CHILD

The Cope Foundation

www.copefoundation.org

Kindermourn

www.kindermourn.org

The Compassionate Friends

www.compassionatefriends.org

Healing Hearts for Bereaved Parents

www.healingheart.net

Share Pregnancy & Infant Loss Support, Inc.

www.nationalshare.org

Center for Loss in Multiple Births
www.climb-support.org

LOSS FROM SUICIDE

American Foundation for Suicide Prevention
www.afsp.org

Friends for Survival, Inc.
www.friendsforsurvival.org

HEARTBEAT
www.heartbeatsurvivorsaftersuicide.org

Sibling Survivors
www.siblingsurvivors.com

LOSS OF A SIBLING

Adult Sibling Grief Community
www.myadultsiblinggrief.com

The Compassionate Friends
www.compassionatefriends.org

Sibling Survivors
www.siblingsurvivors.com

LOSS OF A MILITARY VETERAN

Tragedy Assistance Program for Survivors (TAPS)
www.taps.org

American Widow Project
www.americanwidowproject.org

Military One Source
www.militaryonesource.com

The United Warrior Survivor Foundation
www.neverquitneverforget.org

Gold Star Wives of America, Inc.
www.goldstarwives.org

National Resource Directory
www.nrd.gov

MEMORIAL WEBSITE

www.memorial2u.com

www.imorial.com

www.muchloved.com

CREATIVE & ARTISTIC VISUAL EXPRESSION

The Respite: A Centre for Grief & Hope
www.TheRespite.org

SoulCollage®
www.soulcollage.com

Brave Girls Club
www.bravegirlsclub.com

The Creative Grief Coaching Studio
www.griefcoachingcertification.com

Welcome to Radical Creativity
www.motherhenna.com

CREATIVE DANCE/MOVEMENT

American Dance Therapy Association
www.adta.com

5 Rhythms Global
www.gabrielleroth.com

YOGA FOR GRIEF

Yoga for Grief Relief
www.yogaforgriefrelief.com

Restorative Yoga
www.TheRespite.org

Kripalu: Center for Yoga & Health
www.kripalu.org

MEMORIAL ITEMS/JEWELRY

Expressions of Grief
www.expressionsofgrief.com

My Forever Child
www.myforeverchild.com

Imprint On My Heart
www.imprintonmyheart.com

WRITE A LETTER TO YOUR LOVED ONE

Letterwishes

www.letterwishes.com

ONLINE JOURNAL FOR WIDOWS

Soul Widows

www.soulwidows.org

About the Author

Elizabeth Berrien is the cofounder of the nonprofit The Respite: A Centre for Grief & Hope (www.TheRespite. org) and the Executive Director of Soul Widows (www. SoulWidows.org). a support organization for young widows age 60 and under. She graduated from the University of North Carolina at Asheville in 2004 with an interdisciplinary degree in Human Expression in Culture, with a focus in Anthropology and Dance. She has recently become a Certified Creative Grief Coach®.

With a fresh, personal, and candid voice, Elizabeth takes an integrative approach to the grief journey by incorporating innovative practices she learned through the Model of Heart-Centered Grief. She believes that as people process the loss of a loved one, they should look at themselves as a *whole* person—body, mind, and soul—and that each individual has the ability to access her or his own *creative* path. Through her story of loss and hope, Elizabeth discovered the paradox of grief and joy: namely, a person cannot have one without the other. With relatable wisdom and an edge of humor, she continues to inspire and empower others who are coping with grief by sharing her story, facilitating support groups, writing, and speaking. She resides with her husband and children in Charlotte, North Carolina.

CPSIA information can be obtained at www.ICGtesting.com
Printed in the USA
LVOW11s2345110316

478851LV00002B/34/P